RAINBOW OVER NARRE WARREN

Elsie Johnstone

RAINBOW OVER NARRE WARREN
Elsie Johnstone

Copyright © 2014 by Elsie Johnstone
G. & E. Johnstone Pty. Ltd.
978-0-9925059-1-2

All rights reserved. No part of this publication may be reproduced in any manner whatsoever, or stored in a retrieval system or transmitted in any form or by any means, electronic, mechanical, photocopying, recording or otherwise, without the prior written permission of the authors, except in the case of brief quotations embodied in critical articles or reviews. Please do not participate in or encourage the piracy of copyrighted materials in violation of authors' rights. Purchase only authorized editions.

The publisher and author assume no responsibility or liability whatsoever on the behalf of any purchaser or reader of this material. Any perceived slight of specific people or organizations is unintentional. While all attempts have been made to verify information provided in this publication, neither the author nor the publisher assumes any responsibility for errors, omissions or contrary interpretation of the subject matter herein.

Father John Allen

November 8, 1952 – July 12, 2013

A priest for his people

Appreciation

With thanks to all those family, friends and parishioners who loved and affirmed Father John in his ministry and in his life.

Thank you to the wonderful people at OLHC Narre Warren who helped Father John build the great community it is today.

Special thanks to the fantastic Sister Doreen Dagge and the office staff at OLHC who worked alongside John with such dedication, goodwill and humour. They made things happen.

Grateful thanks to Sister Gail Ryan who was instrumental, as Father John's spiritual advisor, in assisting him in the development and growth of his prayer life. This was crucial to his wellbeing and equilibrium.

Thank you to his fellow priests, clergy and colleagues who embraced and accepted John as their friend and confidante. He enjoyed your affirmation and company. Special mention should be made of John's great mates Father Denis O'Bryan and Father Brendan Hogan who walked graciously with him on his final journey, giving him strength and assurance.

A big thanks to two of John's grand nieces, Kala and Tjala, who provided the inspiration for the wonderful book cover.

To all of those who so generously gave of their time to write down their memories of John and whose contributions made this book possible, I thank you. You wrote from the heart. John would feel so humbled.

- Elsie Johnstone.

"Let us so live that when we come to die, even the undertaker will be sorry."

- Mark Twain.

CONTENTS

A sign in the heavens.. 1
Rainbow over Narre Warren 2
John Damien Allen 5
My path to the priesthood – John's words............ 7
The verses that launched a priestly life................. 31
The prayers John made for his Diaconate............ 43
Ordination – and a big celebration....................... 47
Some famous family 'Johnisms'............................. 49
Father John in the headlines.................................. 59
Sermons linked the gospel and life 63
Photos - John and the extended Allen family........ 75
Father John – a case study...................................... 93
Narre Warren farewells Father John 101
Shocking news, but John accepts it 111
Illness sparks an outpouring of love.................... 115
John finds his way home 143
Final phone messages 149
Thank you God for Father John 153
John penned his last words................................... 155
Photos - Father John, the priest 157
Tribute to a great pilgrim..................................... 165
Genuine and true, John saw everyone's importance. 169
Fond, friendly - and funny - memories of John .. 171
A family remembers 193
Glory and anxiety on and off the footy field....... 221
Obituary, 'The Age' 225
Now that he's gone 229

A sign in the heavens

On a wild, wet and windy July night in 2013 more than 1500 parishioners, family and friends made their way to the church of Our Lady Help of Christians in Narre Warren for the Vigil Mass of Father John Allen, who had died of an insidious cancer just a few days earlier.

About the time Mass was to begin, the storm abated and a magnificent rainbow arched across the sky from one edge of the horizon to the other, casting an ethereal glow over the church below. Was it a sign from above? The symbolic multi-hued ribbon in the sky eventually faded that night. But the memory of Father John remains. This book tells his story.

Rainbow over Narre Warren

When the news came that Father John had died
Narre Warren grieved, the people cried
For they loved this man who walked amongst them
Their spiritual leader but also their friend
He eased their pain in times of sorrow
Assured them of a better tomorrow
Sat with them and held their hands
Assured them of God's bigger plans
He was one of them, he laughed and played
Gave the sacraments, preached and prayed
Ministered to his congregation
Gently leading to salvation
A man of many hues and colours
Leading so that they would follow
Narre Warren parish claimed John its own
A connection between church and home
To honour him they came from work

RAINBOW OVER NARRE WARREN

Through rain and storms to ease their hurt
Gather in church to pray for John
Devastated that he had gone
Then a rainbow arched across the sky
Assuring them John did not die
Instead his life had simply changed
Been exchanged and rearranged
Now he cares in a different way
As they go about their day
Ensuring Our Lady Help of Christians Parish
The place on earth he loved and cherished
Would continue to be a lively place
Blessed by God's amazing grace
Where people gather in grief and love
Form community and feel God above
That sad night when John was laid to rest
This is what that rainbow expressed

- E. J.

John Damien Allen

John Damien Allen was born into a humble fishing family on the Gippsland Lakes in 1952. World War 2 still loomed large in each Australian's immediate memory, and like most people in those days, the family simply put their heads down and worked as hard as they could, happy to put those stressful years behind them.

Jack, John's father, had returned from the war where he had served in the Air Force, married Theresa Bourke from Middle Park and settled in Lakes Entrance where he fished and supplemented his income by gardening and doing odd jobs. The family didn't have much but they had a roof over their heads, plenty of love and lots of fish, so they never went hungry.

By the time John was born things were beginning to get better. Jack began a bait supply business and the couple borrowed money to erect holiday flats on the block next door to their home. They worked diligently to build these two businesses that would sustain the growing family until the day Jack died, feeding, clothing and educating 10 children. "We always had enough and a little bit more. Praise the Lord!" This was Jack's mantra. Theresa and Jack were a hospitable couple who shared whatever they had with whoever happened to turn up at their table.

My path to the priesthood – John's words

After John had been diagnosed and we realized that time was short, I suggested that he tell me his story so that it could be recorded for the family and posterity.

He good-naturedly agreed but as his treatment took effect on his energy levels he started to resist. He was too tired and life was too short. Here is his story in his words and as far as he got.

I was born at Bairnsdale Hospital on the 8th of November 1952, the fifth child and first son of Jack and Theresa Allen of Lakes Entrance. I had four sisters - Margaret, Elsie, Kathleen and Joan.

I was told that it was at a time of big floods and record rains and that the house at Orme Street became separated from the outside dunny by the floodwaters, which stayed up for days. The house became an island and everyone had to take a dinghy to go to the toilet. But Mum was happy; she had her boy.

As was the tradition of the time, on the way home from hospital in the taxi - the family didn't get a car until much later - Mum and Dad called in at the presbytery in Bairnsdale and disturbed Father Frank O'Regan who was having his lunch. This was apparently a big effort because Father loved his food. But he obliged and went over to the church and baptised me during his lunch hour, saving Mum and Dad a trip back to Bairnsdale at a later date. At the time there was no parish and therefore no priest at Lakes Entrance and the priest only came to Lakes once a month to say Mass. Aunty Val and Uncle 'Bud' (David, Dad's only brother) were godparents by proxy.

Father O'Regan was one of the great characters of our diocese. He'd been a good district cricketer before he was ordained and was truly larger than life. After I was ordained he always took the opportunity to tease me by saying, "I baptised you son, so don't let me down young man." Bishop Fox always jokingly backed him up by telling me to take notice, as advice from Father Regan was a form of Benediction.

I don't remember much about my childhood for the first four or five years. I inherited the big cane double pram, as the twins, Kathleen and Joan, were two years older than me. I can remember sitting up happily, enjoying its space, and being taken walking on a Sunday from one end of the town to the other. Elsie says I was like the Maharaja. A Sunday walk was a regular family activity, always with a stop off at the lolly shop for the children and a chat with the locals along the way. There was no television or Sunday sport then so that is what the people of the town did, they went walking.

I can also remember swinging on the front gate between the big hedge that was at the front of the house in Orme Street, waiting for the twins and Margaret and Elsie to come home from school. The only traffic was Hancock's trucks, which left a smell of diesel fumes, a smell that still evokes memories of my childhood. I loved to see Joanie coming home as she had a special, gentle way with her and she was fun.

Home was a pretty happy place. We saw a lot of Dad as he worked from home, catching and selling fishing bait. Our parents got on well and loved each other. There was always plenty of family around - Aunty Val, Uncle Bud and Uncle Dave Allen, all the Carstairs cousins and aunties and also Aunty Etty and the Colemans from Bruthen who were Dad's cousins. Mum's family came from Melbourne to holiday and that was always exciting as she missed them terribly. Sometimes the cousins came alone on the train and would spend a couple of weeks with us.

In winter, I remember going on the bus with Dad to football for the away games. Dad was timekeeper for the Lakes Entrance team and I'd be allowed to sit in the timekeeper's box with him. We went to places like Orbost, Lindenow, Maffra and Stratford. Also places closer to home like Bairnsdale and Bruthen. It was a real big day out. The ladies always brought afternoon tea to us - cakes and sandwiches - and afterwards the footballers would buy me lollies. I suppose I was related to half of them.

One day, in a Lakes versus Orbost game, I accidentally pressed the siren in the last quarter when there was still five minutes to play. Everything stopped. There was panic because there was only a few points in it so poor Dad had to frantically run down to tell the umpire to keep playing out the five minutes. Lakes won! From then on I was never allowed to go anywhere near the siren.

I was always a pretty shy and quiet kid, probably the shyest in the family. I vividly remember my first day at school. It was the very first day St Brendan's School opened in 1957. Father Readman had come around the homes recruiting a few months before, because they needed numbers to start a Catholic school in Lakes. I was only just four - and a bit young to go to school - but my name was put down, even though Mum didn't want me to go that year.

On that first day things were pretty primitive. A couple of partitions converted the church hall into three schoolrooms, one of which was empty. They had a few desks that they got from Orbost, a couple of blackboards that the men knocked up, some chalk and not much else.

It was very overwhelming. When I met Sister Eymard in her nun's habit I ran off home in fright because she looked so strange and different from anything I had ever seen. It took time but I got used to it. We lived diagonally opposite the school but it seemed like a long walk to a little boy. We used to come home for a hot cooked lunch every day. It was Elsie's job to collect me and walk me across the road.

I sat next to Kevin Newman on my first day at school. Other class members included Denise Huggins, my cousin Wendy Allen, Frankie McNamara, Joe Crea, Sammy Cochello and Chris Ramsdell. There were others that came along later.

I enjoyed the nuns, especially Sister Jean and Sister Claude. They were great scouts. Sister Claude was our football coach. She'd get out there in her brown habit and hitch her veil around her big rosary beads that hung from her belt so that it wouldn't fly across her face. She was a tomboy! I barracked for Collingwood like her for a year or two until Father Cusack came along and changed me to Essendon. He bribed us with trips to the footy in Melbourne on the condition that we had to barrack for the Bombers for the day. We got used to barracking for them and so were converted.

Sister Jean taught me for six years and we used to call her 'Old Jeannie'. It was only later that I realized that she was not much older than we were. She was just a young girl of eighteen or nineteen.

They were happy days. My mate 'Turtle' and I did the Nun's messages every night and we chopped their wood for them. We also tidied up if they needed it because we lived near the convent and they could call on us at any time.

Being a Catholic was very much a part of my life from the day I started school. It was a big part of Mum and Dad's life as well, and there were always nuns and priests calling in to chat and drink tea or eat one of Mum's delicious home-cooked meals.

Father Readman was the first of the Australian priests we knew. Before that they had all been Irish. He was a young priest who played football for Lakes Entrance and because of this he did a lot to break down boundaries in the town.

Father Ward was Lakes' first Parish Priest. He was a very sick man and some days he could hardly breathe. He had been in Queensland for four years to try and fix his asthma but came back to the Sale Diocese. When he first came to Lakes he slept in the sacristy while he waited for the presbytery to be built and then he unselfishly moved out of that into a run-down old place on the Esplanade when the nuns arrived.

He was a saintly person. I was an altar boy for a few years, chanting back Latin words I didn't understand. I served the weekday Masses so I'd go to the church at 6.45 am for the 7.00 am Mass. Sometimes Father Ward was too sick with asthma to say Mass so the nuns would send us home, but most mornings he struggled through. He was a lovely, gentle man, but very ill. He was one of the most widely read priests in the state, a prolific reader and his library was amazing. He was my Parish Priest for most of the time that I was growing up. He was at Lakes for 11 years and then went to Yarram in 1967.

I always loved going to church and all the things that happened there and I used to love sitting around after Mass listening to the old fellows talk, all great characters telling their personal stories.

I enjoyed things like helping Dad and the other men in setting up for the dances at Christmas when the school was made back into a hall for six weeks and a band played for the holiday makers every night. I even enjoyed going over with Dad and cleaning up every morning.

I left Lakes in 1966. Dad had had a really good night on the prawns one night and the next morning he said to me, "I think we can manage to send you to boarding school next year, John."

Before this, I was going to go to Nagle College in Bairnsdale, as my older sisters had. But when we went up there to enrol, Mother Catherine who was in charge, said, "I don't think Nagle College is the place for John. He should go to the Brothers." I don't know why. Perhaps Nagle College was too overcrowded and couldn't cater for the science and maths subjects. Any students doing those subjects had to go across to the High School for that and at that stage boys generally studied the science disciplines.

It was a huge decision for Mum and Dad, particularly Mum, as she didn't really want me to go away to school. But Dad saw it as an opportunity that he may have liked when he was young.

So after nine happy years at St Brendan's, I went to St Patrick's College in Sale - run by the Marist Brothers - as a boarder in Year 9 at the age of 13. It was a bit of a jolt being away from family and I never really lived at home after that. I was home for the holidays but that was not the same.

I wasn't really happy about the whole thing. It was a really hot summer day in February 1966 when I fronted up at the college. We had shopped for the uniform at Fords in Bairnsdale and Mum had sewn on all the tags and things. Chris Ramsdell and I were decked out at the same time. It cost an arm and a leg, especially when there were so many children in the family. I needed two blazers, a couple of pairs of trousers, two or three shirts, underwear, sports clothes and one lot of casual clothes that could only be worn on special occasions, like a barbecue down the river. I had never had footy boots before and I had to order them from Mr Coco at his shoe shop, as it was out of season and he had none. Later on Mum posted them to me, each one filled with lollies. I was a hit in the dormitory that night because food was a scarcity at St Pat's.

Dad had recently acquired a new second-hand EK Holden and the trip to Sale was its first long journey. Maureen, Arthur, Eileen and Mary came for the ride. No seat belts then. Robert wasn't born yet. I walked in and was greeted by Brother Crispin whom everyone feared. He was ruthless and could be quite agro, a powerful, over-bearing fellow. But somehow I got on all right with him. I walked up the stairs and he asked, "Hello young fellow, and what is your name?" I told him it was John Allen and he said, "Well, from now on you are going to be known as Joffa, after the great Joffa Allen."

Joffa Allen was a well-known and very popular comedian on television at that stage and that nickname stuck with me all my life. When somebody calls out "Joffa" I immediately know that I went to school with him.

In those days St Pat's had about 200 boarders and 120 day boys, so it was a boarding school that also took local students. The day kids came mainly from Sale, Maffra and Heyfield, while the boarders came from all over Gippsland. There was quite a lot of students from Lakes and Orbost, heaps from Wonthaggi, Leongatha, Koo Wee Rup and places in that area, as well as the odd one or two from Dargo, Omeo, Yarram and Foster.

St Pat's was an old style building with the upstairs dormitories surrounded by a balcony that had been filled in all the way round. There were about 20 to 30 beds to each area and separate dorms for each year level. Our day was very structured. In the morning at 7 am, Brother Lawrence would wake us with a clap and if you didn't spring out of bed he would pull back the covers. He was only a young man at that stage and has since left the brotherhood and married.

The meals were mass-produced and pretty ordinary, not cooked with love like the meals we had at home. However, I did get my revenge later when I went back to Sale to work. I officiated at the funerals of two of the cooks!

The juniors were in bed by 8 pm, but seniors were allowed to stay up later and could listen to music on Radio 3TR.

The brothers had a very disciplined life. They had to be out of bed at 4.30 am for personal prayers. Then they'd get us out of bed and to chapel, followed by breakfast. They had to then teach a full day (no free periods in those days) and after school supervise sport, dinner and homework. They must have fallen into bed absolutely exhausted every night. The majority of the brothers were good men, great fellows who worked very hard. Unfortunately, there were a couple of dubious characters who dragged everyone down with them.

The principal, Brother Jerome, was a great educator who was before his time in a lot of ways. He didn't go along with the old days of bash and crash and used a new, gentle, psychological approach to teaching and managing boys. He was a very good-looking fellow, tall and handsome, a great sportsman who had represented Western Australia in hockey. He was very articulate and personable, taught French and was just a very polished and likable individual. Because he was so gentle a lot of the boys took advantage of him, pushing him to the limits, as boys do. Some of the fellows were very cruel to the younger brothers on the staff, trying their patience and sabotaging their best efforts, pushing some to the edge of breakdown. I suppose it was boys being boys and in a herd situation things can become brutal.

I came from a family of gentle girls and found the first 12 months really difficult. The bullies saw my weakness and honed in on it, targeting me and giving me a hard time. A lot of bullying went on and coming in at Year 9, I was a perfect target. Plus I was a year younger than the other boys at that level. I still resent a couple of the boys who made my life hell. They would mess my bed after I had made it, pinch things from my locker, taunt me, always niggling; they just couldn't leave me alone. I wasn't alone though, there were others. At night you could hear sobbing from other beds in the dormitory as young boys dealt with being away from home and coping with bullies.

However, there were some very good blokes and one day three of them sorted the bullies out and told them if they went anywhere near me again they would be pounded to within an inch of their lives. I was left alone after that because the bullies really were cowards.

The first six months at St Pat's were really raw and hard. We had one Sunday off every month to go home. Just before the first time we were due to go home I had been sick in the infirmary with a bad flu. One night I got delirious and somehow picked up a knife and told another boy who was also in the sick bay to sit back and relax and that I was going to operate on him. Fortunately he was older than me and had no trouble disarming me and putting me back to bed. He is now a doctor himself and when I see him he tells me, "Sit back and relax, I am going to operate on you!"

Because I was sick, the brothers thought I should stay back at the school for the Sunday, but I desperately wanted to go home, so they reluctantly allowed it.

Once I got home, I really didn't want to return to College. Mum would have pulled the plug there and then and let me go to school locally. But Dad insisted I go back. There were four or five of us Lakes kids attending St Pat's and the parents all car-pooled, taking turns to pick us up and drop us back in time for Benediction. Dad won out and that weekend I was taken back to school in style in the Crea's big limousine.

When I got back I was still quite sick but Brother Jerome said, "You told me you were well enough to go home, so that's the end of the infirmary for you. Back to lessons tomorrow." I somehow made it through.

I don't think I enjoyed boarding school like my brother Arthur did later. I felt helpless and things happened around me that I had no control over. I missed home and all the things that were going on there that I wanted to be a part of and just couldn't. It was just like this cancer I have at the moment. It leaves me feeling powerless.

I repeated Matriculation in 1970. The previous year I had been a year younger than everybody else, having started school at only four years old. I really enjoyed my second year as I had matured and was the same age as everybody else. At last I had the opportunity to play cricket and footy for the college which was great. We swam in the river and had outings to the beach at Seaspray every St Patrick's Day. Nobody ever drowned.

Overall I went to school with a great bunch of fellows - all sorts, some high achievers and others just characters. I have visited some of them in my role as a prison chaplain.

The temptation to run away from school proved too strong for some. One fellow cleared off one day and they never found him for 10 months. By that time he was up in Queensland. And over the time a couple of boys went home for the holidays and didn't come back because they had suffered some misadventure. That was sobering, as we knew everybody well.

I remember one night hearing on the radio news that there had been a railway crossing accident at Welshpool and after that finding out the victim was the dad of two of the boys. That news cast a real gloom over the place.

One time we prepared the College oval for a Hawthorn practice game. Brother Crispin was so proud of its condition that he had his photo taken alongside of it with a story in the paper. The night before the big match the cows got onto the pitch and rendered it unusable.

As I progressed through school the rules loosened and we were allowed to go home for special events – hitch hike even! We got home the best way we could and Hancock's truck drivers would always pick us up because they knew why we were on the road and they were heading our way.

In hindsight St Pat's opened me up to many more opportunities than if I had stayed in Lakes. It opened my eyes to other people from other places with other dreams and hopes. It gave me chances I wouldn't have otherwise had.

I first started to think about becoming a priest at a time during the Vietnam War when a fellow called Brian Ross from Orbost, a conscientious objector, was jailed in the Sale Prison for his beliefs. There were demonstrations every week outside the jail in support of him. We used to wander down there for the excitement. Brother Jerome threatened us with detention because we weren't supposed to be off the school property, but we enjoyed the jostle.

This day the wind was blowing from the southeast and it was raining hard. A big sign was painted on the jail wall saying, 'Free Brian Ross'. The peaceful demonstration began to get violent.

Father Bill Deery, a young assistant priest at Sale was standing next to me. He said, "It's a pity they haven't read Chapters 5, 6, and 7 of Matthew's gospel."

I nodded, but I had never read it and didn't have a clue what he was talking about. I went back to the college library and looked up the chapters and discovered they were about the Sermon on the Mount - loving your enemies, turning the other cheek, caring for those who have less. The demonstrators who had caused the disturbance were not really about peace; they were as bad as those they protested about. (See following, Matthew Chapters 5 – 7.)

About three weeks later Father Deery asked two or three of us if we would be interested in helping as a catechetic leader in weekly group discussions at the local Technical School. I knew most of the fellows as they had previously been students at St Pat's but had changed to the Tech to learn a trade. I jumped at the chance because it meant that we got out of an hour of school, plus Bill took us out to lunch afterwards. Decent food!

At the end of my school days I was unsure of what I wanted to do. Initially I studied teaching for six months at Melbourne Secondary Teachers' College. This came to an abrupt halt when I went on my first teaching round and thought, "I can't stand this. This is not for me." So I left there. The only thing that was exceptional about teachers' college was that I was in the same tutorial group as 'Crackers' Keenan, the Melbourne footballer. He left as well.

I then applied for a job at St Vincent's Hospital where I worked for nine months. They offered me a cadetship to do hospital management but I was not convinced and I knew that there were other blokes who were desperate to do that so I quit and applied for a job at the bank in Sale, which I got.

By this time Dad was getting pretty agitated about my unsettled work life. He was not happy, doubting my work ethic and lack of commitment. But I was holding back because in my heart I knew what I should be doing.

One night I went to see Father Gerard Coffey at the Sale presbytery. I told him I wanted to be a priest but that I would work for 12 months before I joined up. He insisted that I not wait and instead go to the seminary intake that was beginning studies the following week. I went home to Lakes to break the news.

Mum was over the moon. She was Irish enough to think it was a great blessing to have a priest in the family. Dad was not so happy because he could see a lot of pitfalls in the life I had chosen.

I needed a reference from my Parish Priest before I could go any further, but I had a bit of a problem getting it from the P. P. at the time, Father Rowe. He was feuding with everyone in Lakes at that stage. The men of the parish, Dad amongst them, had been to the Bishop on a delegation regarding his behaviour and Father Rowe was not a happy man.

One summer's day, I approached him requesting the reference. He never invited me in or let me pass the front door, immediately declaring, "I'm not giving you a reference. You're an Allen and you'll up and leave the seminary and my name will be mud all over Victoria. I've got to think of my own good name, so you're not getting one." What could I say?

I drove back to Sale, knocked on the Bishop's door and when Father Coffey answered I told him, "I have some bad news. Father Rowe won't give me a reference." Bishop Fox poked his head out from behind the door and said, "If Father Rowe won't give you a reference, John Allen, that's good enough reference for me."

I started at the seminary in Werribee on the 27th February 1972. I found it much easier than boarding school because we had more freedom and autonomy and besides I'd lived away from home since I was 13 years old. Twenty-one men and boys began their studies, and in the end, only seven were ordained.

Mum and Dad brought me down from Lakes. We stopped for petrol at Trafalgar and Monsignor Crowe was filling up his car at the garage there.

"I hear your son is going into the seminary, Jack," he said.

"Yes, I hope he goes okay." Dad was still a bit uncertain.

"Don't worry Jack. He'll go well. All you have to do is to consult the Stud Book and in his case it looks magnificent. The genetics are good." Dad laughed. But then the 'Mons' turned to me and said, "Whatever you do, don't commit to good friends until the last couple of years. Be wary. There are a lot of fellows who go to the seminary who shouldn't be there. They go for the wrong reasons, so be careful."

The diocese paid for all my educational expenses although it still cost Mum and Dad plenty. I worked the semester holidays each year pulling beer at the Bruthen Hotel, owned by Betty and Matt Martino who were very good and supportive to me all my time in the seminary.

In joining the priesthood my reasons were simple. I simply wanted to make a difference in the world and thought that preaching the Gospel was the way to do it. I really had no other motives.

After a long journey from Lakes Entrance we enjoyed a big afternoon tea with seminarians, Cardinal Knox and the bishops. My little brother Robert had a great time and managed to scoff practically all the cream cakes on one of the tables.

For the first few months I shared a room with Joe Ruys in the grand old mansion on the Werribee River where the rooms were huge, cold and bare. In the summer it was great but in the winter it was freezing. We swam daily in the river in summer and played football on the polo field. The grounds were beautiful.

We rose at 6 am, went to Chapel at 6.30 am for prayer and Mass, then ate breakfast. Three mornings a week we'd be treated to black pudding and poached eggs because the Irish nuns who cooked and kept house for us thought it was good for us. They were called the Cluny Sisters – the Sisters of St Joseph of Cluny. We students did the washing up, setting up, and all of the outside jobs.

Classes for the day started at 9 am. We were taught by the Jesuits and in first year studied scripture and philosophy. After morning classes we had lunch, then worked and took part in recreational activities. I played in the football team against the other universities and the big game of the year was the Theologians v. Philosophers, always umpired by Don Jolley, who was a top league umpire at the time.

Tea was followed by study and prayer. All in all it was a very monastic style of life. It was difficult for some and a couple left at different stages. Boarding school had prepared me for the seminary.

As it happened 1972 was the last year that the seminary operated from the mansion at Werribee. In 1973 the college transferred to brand new premises at Clayton. It was a state-of-the-art, architecturally designed, purpose-built building. It was quite beautiful in a 60s way but with no regard for disability access and things that would be required today.

As students we were given much more freedom and flexibility to come and go in the community. We studied at university with mainstream students coming home at night to our small group of seven seminarians who shared prayers and meals. I got on well with everyone because coming from a large family I had learnt to get on and mix with people. I enjoyed the fact that it was just like a family home. This modern model was much more humane.

Dennis Crameri and I started a football team that joined the YCW competition and with a few outside recruits we went onto win the premiership in 1977. (Graeme Johnstone has a piece about this match later in the book.)

Dad and Mum were a long way away and still had young children, so they could only get down to

Melbourne on special occasions. Because Lakes Entrance was a holiday place, my friends and colleagues often called in at home in Orme Street, and so they got to know people who worked and studied with me.

In the meantime, Aunty Agnes, Uncle Bill and their family, Aunty Eily, and my sisters, Elsie and Marg and brothers-in-law Graeme and Bryan and their families filled the gaps, coming to my celebrations and events.

At the end of six years I was ordained a deacon - on the day Collingwood played North Melbourne in the Grand Final replay of 1977! We had deliberately set the date for the week after that year's Grand Final, so there would be no clash, but the drawn match disrupted our plans. The seminary's rector stayed away because he had two brothers playing in that match.

It was also a time of upheaval in the church and much questioning was going on. In his sermon Bishop Fox took the opportunity to accuse the seminary staff of being heretics for what they were teaching us students. He had failed to move forward after Vatican 2 and was living in the past. In reply Father Shanley, the P. P. at Lakes Entrance, grabbed the microphone and praised the seminary staff for the job they had done in producing modern priests to take the place of old fogies like the bishop and himself. He didn't care about repercussions.

Afterwards the ladies of the parish put on a reception for a huge crowd in the Mechanics Hall.

I love all the traditions of the church and enjoy the rituals. I have never been anti-authority so have accepted what my bishops have decreed.

Once ordained a deacon, which means 'to serve', I could marry, baptise and preach. We now have married deacons in the church; in fact we have Deacon Peter Stringfellow at Narre Warren who does a marvellous job.

I became the first deacon in our diocese to live in a parish to gain experience of parish life. I was part of a pilot program that the seminary wanted to set up. Dear old Bishop Fox wasn't going to have anything so revolutionary in his diocese so I ended up living in East Preston for 12 months in the presbytery with an Irishman called Father Tony Cleary. It gave me a great insight into what my life as a priest could be, and I loved it. Tony was a lovely man - educated, loved his music, cultured but shy. He was a real priest for his people, allowing people to take charge and do things; he gave them autonomy. It was their parish and he was the facilitator and guide.

Father Terry Kean was his assistant, another very good man. They both worked bloody hard. East Preston was a rough and very poor place, on the edge of the old Olympic Village that had been built for the 1956 games that were held in Melbourne. The government had dismantled the slums in the inner city and transferred the poor people there. There was also a solid, middle-class section of parishioners who lived on or towards the hill. This resulted in a divided parish.

With the help of the nuns the church ran youth groups and organized welfare for families who, for one reason or another, were unable to cope. There were many single parent families, some had husbands in jail, while a lot of the husbands who were home abused their wives. Life was tough. The nuns provided support and care for families and did the best they could to ensure the children weren't hungry.

Still, it was a great parish. They had a large youth group and a wonderful choir that sang every Sunday and brought the Mass alive. People came from all around to enjoy the music.

While there I also worked at Winlaton Youth Training Centre, an extremely sad place. It was a government owned and run female youth correctional facility, located on 18 acres in Nunawading, designed to accommodate 14 to 18 year old wards of the state. Most of them were just frightened little kids who had been caught doing something stupid and had been made wards of the state. Some girls felt safer there than they did in their own homes. Some would escape just to avoid the possibility of being sent back home into an abusive situation.

As part of my ministry I visited their families and got to know them too. Unfortunately, the mums were often downtrodden and abused as well. It was a generational cycle that was hard to escape.

It was here that I learnt the value of knocking on doors and talking to people. There were some knock-backs but I was usually made welcome as the people loved the church because, at that time, the church cared for them. It was good to be Catholic in their situation. If a bloke was in jail he put his name down as Catholic, whether he was or not, because the church's social services would look after the families. Our team at East Preston was working hard with people who were struggling at the bottom of the ladder. We had no time to question the larger church; we simply left that to the big boys.

I modelled my whole priestly life on the East Preston experience, where the church came to the people and tended to them according to their needs. I never wanted to be a bishop. I just wanted to be a good priest who enjoyed the people around me.

Since then, for me, the welfare of my parishioners has always been at the centre of my ministry and that is what I always concentrated on. I love the Gospel and I wanted to make a difference in the world.

The verses that launched a priestly life

The following scripture is the Gospel reading that was pointed out to John during an anti-Vietnam demonstration he was observing one day. On reading these words, he was so impressed, it started him on his journey towards the priesthood.

Matthew 5-7

The Beatitudes

When Jesus saw the crowds, he went up the mountain; and after he sat down, his disciples came to him. Then he began to speak, and taught them, saying:

"Blessed are the poor in spirit, for theirs is the kingdom of heaven.

"Blessed are those who mourn, for they will be comforted.

"Blessed are the meek, for they will inherit the earth.

"Blessed are those who hunger and thirst for righteousness, for they will be filled.

"Blessed are the merciful, for they will receive mercy.

"Blessed are the pure in heart, for they will see God.

"Blessed are the peacemakers, for they will be called children of God.

"Blessed are those who are persecuted for righteousness' sake, for theirs is the kingdom of heaven.

"Blessed are you when people revile you and persecute you and utter all kinds of evil against you falsely on my account. Rejoice and be glad, for your reward is great in heaven, for in the same way they persecuted the prophets who were before you."

Salt and light

"You are the salt of the earth; but if salt has lost its taste, how can its saltiness be restored? It is no longer good for anything, but is thrown out and trampled under foot.

"You are the light of the world. A city built on a hill cannot be hidden. No one after lighting a lamp puts it under the bushel basket, but on the lamp stand, and it gives light to all in the house. In the same way, let your light shine before others, so that they may see your good works and give glory to your Father in heaven."

The law and the prophets

"Do not think that I have come to abolish the law or the prophets; I have come not to abolish but to fulfil. For truly I tell you, until heaven and earth pass away, not one letter, not one stroke of a letter, will pass from the law until all is accomplished. "Therefore, whoever breaks one of the least of these commandments, and teaches others to do the same, will be called least in the kingdom of heaven; but whoever does them and teaches them will be called great in the kingdom of heaven. For I tell you, unless your righteousness exceeds that of the scribes and Pharisees, you will never enter the kingdom of heaven."

Concerning anger

"You have heard that it was said to those of ancient times, 'You shall not murder.' And, 'Whoever murders shall be liable to judgment.' But I say to you that if you are angry with a brother or sister, you will be liable to judgment; and if you insult a brother or sister, you will be liable to the council; and if you say, 'You fool', you will be liable to the hell of fire. So when you are offering your gift at the altar, if you remember that your brother or sister has something against you, leave your gift there before the altar and go; first be reconciled to your brother or sister, and then come and offer your gift. Come to terms quickly with your accuser while you are on the way to court with him, or your accuser may hand you over to the judge, and the judge to the guard, and you will be thrown into prison. Truly I tell you, you will never get out until you have paid the last penny."

Concerning adultery

"You have heard that it was said, 'You shall not commit adultery.' But I say to you that everyone who looks at a woman with lust has already committed adultery with her in his heart. If your right eye causes you to sin, tear it out and throw it away; it is better for you to lose one of your members than for your whole body to be thrown into hell. And if your right hand causes you to sin, cut it off and throw it away; it is better for you to lose one of your members than for your whole body to go into hell."

Concerning divorce

"It was also said, 'Whoever divorces his wife, let him give her a certificate of divorce.' But I say to you that anyone who divorces his wife, except on the ground of unchastity, causes her to commit adultery; and whoever marries a divorced woman commits adultery."

Concerning oaths

"Again, you have heard that it was said to those of ancient times, 'You shall not swear falsely, but carry out the vows you have made to the Lord.' But I say to you, do not swear at all, either by heaven, for it is the throne of God, or by the earth, for it is his footstool, or by Jerusalem, for it is the city of the great King. And do not swear by your head, for you cannot make one hair white or black. Let your word be 'Yes, yes' or 'No, no.' Anything more than this comes from the evil one."

Concerning retaliation

"You have heard that it was said, 'An eye for an eye and a tooth for a tooth.' But I say to you, do not resist an evildoer. But if anyone strikes you on the right cheek, turn the other also; and if anyone wants to sue you and take your coat, give your cloak as well; and if anyone forces you to go one mile, go also the second mile. Give to everyone who begs from you, and do not refuse anyone who wants to borrow from you."

Love for enemies

"You have heard that it was said, 'You shall love your neighbour and hate your enemy.' But I say to you, love your enemies and pray for those who persecute you, so that you may be children of your Father in heaven; for he makes his sun rise on the evil and on the good, and sends rain on the righteous and on the unrighteous. For if you love those who love you, what reward do you have? Do not even the tax collectors do the same? And if you greet only your brothers and sisters, what more are you doing than others? Do not even the Gentiles do the same? Be perfect, therefore, as your heavenly Father is perfect."

Concerning almsgiving

"Beware of practising your piety before others in order to be seen by them; for then you have no reward from your Father in heaven.

"So whenever you give alms, do not sound a trumpet before you, as the hypocrites do in the synagogues and in the streets, so that they may be praised by others. Truly I tell you, they have received their reward. But when you give alms, do not let your left hand know what your right hand is doing, so that your alms may be done in secret; and your Father who sees in secret will reward you."

Concerning prayer

"And whenever you pray, do not be like the hypocrites; for they love to stand and pray in the synagogues and at the street corners, so that they may be seen by others. Truly I tell you, they have received their reward. But whenever you pray, go into your room and shut the door and pray to your Father who is in secret; and your Father who sees in secret will reward you.

"When you are praying, do not heap up empty phrases as the Gentiles do; for they think that they will be heard because of their many words. Do not be like them, for your Father knows what you need before you ask him.

"Pray then in this way:

> *Our Father in heaven,*
> *Hallowed be your name.*
> *Your kingdom come.*
> *Your will be done,*
> *On earth as it is in heaven.*
> *Give us this day our daily bread.*
> *And forgive us our debts,*
> *As we also have forgiven our debtors.*
> *And do not bring us to the time of trial,*
> *But rescue us from the evil one.*

"For if you forgive others their trespasses, your heavenly Father will also forgive you; but if you do not forgive others, neither will your Father forgive your trespasses."

Concerning fasting

"And whenever you fast, do not look dismal, like the hypocrites, for they disfigure their faces so as to show others that they are fasting. Truly I tell you, they have received their reward. But when you fast, put oil on your head and wash your face, so that your fasting may be seen not by others but by your Father who is in secret; and your Father who sees in secret will reward you."

Concerning treasures

"Do not store up for yourselves treasures on earth, where moth and rust consume and where thieves break in and steal; but store up for yourselves treasures in heaven, where neither moth nor rust consumes and where thieves do not break in and steal.

"For where your treasure is, there your heart will be also."

The sound eye

"The eye is the lamp of the body. So, if your eye is healthy, your whole body will be full of light; but if your eye is unhealthy, your whole body will be full of darkness. If then the light in you is darkness, how great is the darkness!"

Serving two masters

"No one can serve two masters; for a slave will either hate the one and love the other, or be devoted to the one and despise the other. You cannot serve God and wealth."

Do not worry

"Therefore I tell you, do not worry about your life, what you will eat or what you will drink, or about your body, what you will wear. Is not life more than food, and the body more than clothing? Look at the birds of the air; they neither sow nor reap nor gather into barns, and yet your heavenly Father feeds them. Are you not of more value than they? And can any of you by worrying add a single hour to your span of life? And why do you worry about clothing? Consider the lilies of the field, how they grow; they neither toil nor spin, yet I tell you, even Solomon in all his glory was not clothed like one of these. But if God so clothes the grass of the field, which is alive today and tomorrow is thrown into the oven, will he not much more clothe you - you of little faith? Therefore do not worry, saying, 'What will we eat?' or 'What will we drink?' or 'What will we wear?' For it is the Gentiles who strive for all these things; and indeed your heavenly Father knows that you need all these things. But strive first for the kingdom of God and his righteousness, and all these things will be given to you as well.

"So do not worry about tomorrow, for tomorrow will bring worries of its own. Today's trouble is enough for today."

Judging others

"Do not judge, so that you may not be judged. For with the judgment you make you will be judged, and the measure you give will be the measure you get. Why do you see the speck in your neighbour's eye, but do not notice the log in your own eye? Or how can you say to your neighbour, 'Let me take the speck out of your eye,' while the log is in your own eye? You hypocrite, first take the log out of your own eye, and then you will see clearly to take the speck out of your neighbour's eye."

Profaning the holy

"Do not give what is holy to dogs; and do not throw your pearls before swine, or they will trample them under foot and turn and maul you."

Ask, search, knock

"Ask, and it will be given to you; search, and you will find; knock, and the door will be opened for you. For everyone who asks receives, and everyone who searches finds, and for everyone who knocks, the door will be opened. Is there anyone among you who, if your child asks for bread, will give a stone? Or if the child asks for a fish, will give a snake? If you then, who are evil, know how to give good gifts to your children, how much more will your Father in heaven give good things to those who ask him!"

The golden rule

"In everything do to others as you would have them do to you; for this is the law and the prophets."

The narrow gate

"Enter through the narrow gate; for the gate is wide and the road is easy that leads to destruction, and there are many who take it. For the gate is narrow and the road is hard that leads to life, and there are few who find it."

A tree and its fruit

"Beware of false prophets, who come to you in sheep's clothing but inwardly are ravenous wolves. You will know them by their fruits. Are grapes gathered from thorns, or figs from thistles? In the same way, every good tree bears good fruit, but the bad tree bears bad fruit. A good tree cannot bear bad fruit, nor can a bad tree bear good fruit. Every tree that does not bear good fruit is cut down and thrown into the fire. Thus you will know them by their fruits."

Concerning self-deception

"Not everyone who says to me, 'Lord, Lord,' will enter the kingdom of heaven, but only one who does the will of my Father in heaven. On that day many will say to me, 'Lord, Lord, did we not prophesy in your name, and cast out demons in your name, and do many deeds of power in your name?' Then I will declare to them, 'I never knew you; go away from me, you evildoers.' "

Hearers and doers

"Everyone then who hears these words of mine and acts on them will be like a wise man who built his house on rock. The rain fell, the floods came, and the winds blew and beat on that house, but it did not fall, because it had been founded on rock.

"And everyone who hears these words of mine and does not act on them will be like a foolish man who built his house on sand. The rain fell, and the floods came, and the winds blew and beat against that house, and it fell - and great was its fall!"

Now when Jesus had finished saying these things, the crowds were astounded at his teaching, for he taught them as one.

The prayers John made for his Diaconate

These are the prayers devised by John on the occasion of his ordination to a Deacon at St Brendan's Parish Church, Lakes Entrance, on 1/10/1977.

Prayer of surrender

I surrender myself to you, oh Lord, and ask you to put an end to my restlessness.

I give my will.

I do not believe any longer that I am so intelligent that I can understand myself, my life or other men. Teach me to think your thoughts.

I give you my plans

I do not believe any longer that my life finds meaning in what I reach through my plans. I entrust myself to your plan, for you know me best.

My anxiety about other men I give to you.

I do not believe any longer that with my anxiety I can improve anything. That remains with you. Why should I be anxious?

My anxiety about the power of others I give to you.

You were powerless before the almighty. The almighty have fallen. You live.

My fear of my own failures I give to you.

I do not have to be a successful man if I wish to be one blessed according to your will.

All insolvable questions, all discontent with myself, all my cramped hopes I give to you. I give up running into locked doors and wait for you. You will open them.

I give you myself. I belong to you Lord. You have me in your hand. I thank you.

Thank you note

This is John's Diaconate thank you note that he wrote for the many family and friends who gathered to help him celebrate a very special day.

Dear Friends,

I will take this opportunity to thank you for making this day such a special one for me. There are quite a few people who need to be thanked for the time they have put into organizing this day.

First of all, Bishop Fox, for giving me permission to have this ordination in my parish church and for travelling from Sale to perform the ceremony.

Also, my Mum and Dad who have helped me so much down through the years, for the love they have shown to each other and also to me, and for the faith they have passed on to me.

To Greg, my cousin and friend for typing this program and being such a great support to me during our time in the seminary together.

To my brothers and sisters, for their support and concern all of my life.

To Father Shanley, Sister Mary and Veronica and Frank Neaves, for putting time into the music for this big day.

To the people of East Preston, who have in many ways adopted me and have taught me to give service.

Also to the Ladies of the Parish, who have done a lot of hard work organizing the luncheon.

Lastly (but not by any means least) my fellow students, the Cluny Sisters and the priests on the staff of the 'Mighty Corpus' for being such good fun and for making my seminary years happy ones and for helping me along the 'way'.

Shalom,
John.

Ordination – and a big celebration

Thanksgiving ceremony at Lakes Entrance

It was a memorable day in the history of St Brendan's Catholic Church, Lakes Entrance, and for the parishioners when Father John Allen celebrated a Thanksgiving Mass on August 20th.

Father Allen, who is the first resident of Lakes Entrance to be ordained to the priesthood, is the eldest son of Mr and Mrs Jack Allen of Lakes Entrance and was educated by the Sisters of St Joseph at St Brendan's School and by the Marist College, Sale.

He has studied for the priesthood at Corpus Christi College at Werribee and Clayton since 1972 and during the intervening years he has worked in East Preston and Maffra parishes and at Winlaton Girls Training Centre.

Ordination at Sale

The Ordination by the Bishop of Sale, the Most Reverend A. F. Fox, took place at St Mary's Cathedral at Sale on August 19th.

The following day the Lakes Entrance Mechanics Hall was the setting for the Thanksgiving Mass and reception for 500 relatives and friends representing many areas of Gippsland.

Assisting Father Allen as con-celebrants of the Mass were Reverend Father Shanley, Parish Priest of Lakes Entrance, Dean J. Readman of Sale and Reverend Father Cusack of Trafalgar, both of whom had served at Lakes Entrance; Right Reverend Monsignor S. Crowe, formerly of Bairnsdale, Reverend Father T Keane and Reverend Father B. Glashen of Melbourne.

Sister Veronica, Sister Mary and Mr Frank Neaves arranged the musical program for the Mass and the Cantor was Michael Cashman. Children from St Brendan's School assisted with musical accompaniment and made the posters that decorated the hall.

Presentation from Parish

During the afternoon tea, provided and served by the ladies of St Brendan's Parish, opportunity was taken to make a presentation to Father Allen.

Mr Ray Kleinitz and Mr Arthur Williams, on behalf of the parishioners of Lakes Entrance, asked him to accept the gift of a car.

Reverend Father Allen has returned to Corpus Christi College until the end of 1978 when he will be appointed as an assistant to a parish in the Diocese of Sale.

- *Bairnsdale Advertiser, 23/08/1978.*

Some famous family 'Johnisms'

John had his own little special foibles that made him so endearing. I have some tales of John that have become part of family folklore.

Squash court blockade

John was born a mollydooker, that is, he was left-handed. As was common practice in those days, the good nuns attempted to alter his hand orientation and have him write with his right hand.

Consequently in some things John was ambidextrous and this came in very handy on the squash court. He was a very frustrating opponent as he would place that big frame of his squarely in the middle of the court and simply change the racquet from one hand to the other. It saved him chasing the ball. His opponent would come off the court a lather of sweat and John would invariably have won the game with hardly expending any energy at all.

Cure for shyness

Because he was a shy child, Therese thought it would be good for John to learn to play a musical instrument - the banjo. No particular reason for the choice of that instrument other than his cousin Anne-Marie Butt was learning to play banjo and she was doing very well.

Because John was a left-handed he needed a left-handed banjo, which was not easy to come by in Lakes Entrance in the 1950s. But Therese was determined and managed to acquire one. Music teachers were also a rarity but there was a very old lady called Mrs Jamieson who had taught a couple of generations of piano players in the town and who played the organ at St Nicholas' Church of England. After negotiations she reluctantly agreed to teach John banjo. He had attended four lessons when she dropped dead ...

As a result, he could only play one tune, 'God Save the Queen'! For years there was an abandoned left-handed banjo in the top cupboard at Orme Street. To add insult to injury, the national anthem was changed in the 1970s to 'Advance Australia Fair', so John's brief foray into music amounted to absolutely nothing.

A playmate's role

John was a boy born after four girls and then he had a sister Maureen come next on the scene. That is probably the beginnings of his adult persona as a people person; he had been brought up in a gentle atmosphere where dialogue and co-operation was king. He knew from an early age that he wanted to be a priest and his favourite playtime was to convert mother Theresa's dressing table into an altar using holy pictures and household items to approximate a chalice, a bible, candles and other religious paraphernalia. He would don a sheet for a surplice, turn his back on the congregation, as was the practice before Vatican 2, and incant in an unintelligible language to approximate Latin. Of course he needed an altar boy and that is where Maureen came in handy!

Theresa's new model

Because John was born a couple of years after the twins he inherited their giant, woven-cane, twin pram as his transport. He occupied it proudly like the Pope does the pope-mobile, especially every Sunday after the weekly roast when the family dressed up and went for a walk around the town. One Sunday the family was walking down the main street near the footbridge and the Bruthen relations pulled up in their brand new Nash Rambler, honked the horn and jumped out eager to talk about it. "Have you seen our new model?" they said. Theresa was not impressed. "Have you seen *my* new model?" she enquired, smiling lovingly at John who was beaming his big smile in the twin pram. Theresa preferred her 'little fat man' to all the flash cars in Australia.

(Here is reference to that event in a much longer poem brother-in-law Graeme Johnstone wrote for a family gathering to celebrate John's 50th birthday.)

> *Down the Esplanade one day*
> *In their new Rambler V8*
> *The wealthy cousins did sashay*
> *"It's plush and it goes just great!"*
> *Dear Theresa was not over-awed*
> *She smiled like a Cheshire cat*
> *Squeezing little Johnny by the arm*
> *She said, "Feel the upholstery on that!"*

The boat sank

When John was about three years old the family was up the lake in the boat for a picnic. Jack had taken a dinghy load of kids ashore and was on the return trip for the rest of us when John went overboard. Barely a splash! He just disappeared over the side of the boat and we could see him lying on the sandy bottom of the clear lake. Mum couldn't swim, but that didn't stop her. She dropped Maureen, the baby she was feeding at the time, and went clean over after him in her overcoat. Dad rescued the both of them. John was put in recovery position on the engine box and the water gushed out of his lungs. He opened his eyes, saw his dripping wet mother and said, "The boat sank and Mummy got wet."

RAINBOW OVER NARRE WARREN

(Here is another excerpt from Graeme Johnstone's birthday poem.)

A boating picnic at the Barrier one day
Struck a nasty chord
There were panic stations all around
When Johnny went overboard!

Down, down, down he went
Nestling in the reeds
Theresa didn't have a chance
To go for the Rosary beads ...

Barbecue king

When John was the curate at Traralgon, the family Christmas party was held there. On this particular Christmas, the 'must have' summer accessory was the newly released Weber barbecue, a coal-burning kettle oven that could cook large lumps of meat in an interesting and succulent fashion. The older siblings agreed that it was just what Mum needed to feed the hoards in a trouble-free manner - because the cooking would be done outside and Dad would be doing most of the work.

The plan was that after the Christmas barbecue was cooked and Mum and Dad had declared how delicious everything was, we would tell them that the Weber was theirs, a gift to love and cherish. We girls were bringing the meat but this type of kettle needed to be fired up early and the coals allowed to burn down, so we asked John to read the instructions carefully and do that task in between Sunday Masses. He tried his very best! But we got there to find a very frustrated John complaining that the fire kept going out. Of course it did. He had lit the coal not in the kettle, but in the tray underneath that was meant to collect the ash! We ended up going down the street and buying take-away roast chickens that day.

The famous flat spin

John was a very placid child and slow to anger. But when he did get angry it was a sight to behold. He would drop to the floor on his back, furiously kicking and screaming while spinning in circles. Everyone would keep a safe distance until he calmed down. This action went down in family folklore as 'John's flat spin'. One particular day he and Mum were in Bairnsdale, probably on a doctor's pregnancy visit for the next child. The heat and the shopping got to John during the busy lunchtime rush and he blew up in the middle of Coles. In those days all Coles stores were set up with a centre counter that had pathways around it. John dropped to the floor in a raging flat spin right at the point where nobody could pass. He stopped the traffic in Bairnsdale that day.

A little tipple fixes every problem

When John was at the seminary in Clayton he offered to baby-sit our eldest child Caitlin while my husband and I went out to dinner. He felt confident that he had always been around children and that he could do the job easily. We enjoyed our first post-baby outing and came home to find John calmly watching late night television and Caitlin sound asleep in her cot.

When I congratulated him he said it hadn't been easy in the beginning as the baby had cried endlessly and nothing he could do would soothe her. In desperation he phoned our Aunty Eily who was the font of all knowledge. Even though she had never had children herself she was everybody's favourite aunt and she was happy to give some good old homespun advice: "Give her a teaspoon of brandy."

So he did - and she slept like a baby.

Trouble was that I didn't as I kept checking her all night to make sure she was still alive. John never offered to baby sit again.

When four is the new three

One weekend the Johnstone family went to stay with John at Yarram, his first parish as P.P. The children didn't mind going to the Saturday night Mass but when I asked them to line up again the next morning they were not convinced they needed to go twice in a weekend. I explained that we were staying with John and that it would be the right thing to do.

"Okay," said the youngest reluctantly, "I will go, but I won't listen to him."

At that Mass, John preached about a lighthouse and how it protected the sailors with its light. He was probably nervous because we were there and in his effort to impress he declared that from this story there were "three things we needed to learn." He held up his fingers to illustrate the point. Only trouble was that he held up four of them! The children had fun teasing him about that for the rest of his life.

An act of contrition

John was on his annual holiday with fellow priests on the Gold Coast when he got caught in a rip. He tried to swim across it but was getting carried further and further out to sea. He thought he was a goner. Out of the blue a friendly surfer saw him, gathered him onto his surfboard, paddled him to the beach and set him down. He had to walk back a couple of kilometres or so to where he had first disappeared. His priestly mates were all mightily relieved when he finally turned up.

That night at dinner he was recalling his adventure when he was asked if, as he was being carried away to his death, he had said an Act of Contrition.

"I tried to," said John, "but all I could think of was Grace before Meals!"

As much as he could do

John loved his food and sitting at the dinner table with good food, company and conversation was the place he most liked to be. The funny thing is that he never learnt to cook. He could make a cup of tea and butter bread but that was about the extent of it. His mother, sisters and housekeepers all made sure he was well fed and watered.

Because he was a priest who liked to visit the families in his parish he spent many meals as the guest at other people's tables and because he was a welcome guest they always went the extra mile, serving sweets and rich foods. Consequently he constantly struggled with his weight. But he did try! He walked every day and when he was at home he kept a strict eye on his calorie intake. Still he remained rotund.

One day when one of his sisters expressed concern about his weight he declared, "I am what I am. I can't walk any further or eat any less!"

Still thinking of others

John died on the 12th July and my birthday is the 16th July. On that day I answered a knock at the door to take delivery of a pot of beautiful white orchids that John had arranged from hospital. Even on his deathbed he had found time to think of others. I will think of him every year when they bloom. Such a dear, sweet man.

Father John in the headlines

*Ex-classmates gather to celebrate
Silver Jubilee to Priesthood*

MORWELL – A reunion of old friends to celebrate the Silver Jubilee of Narre Warren parish priest Fr John Allen was held in Morwell on August 29.

Some 25 of Fr John's classmates from the matriculation classes of 1969 and 1970 at St Patrick's College Sale and friends of old gathered to congratulate him for 25 years of generous and faithful service to the priesthood.

Master of ceremonies Brendan 'Gus' Clifford welcomed everyone to an evening of reminiscing and renewing old acquaintances.

Mark Murphy, representing the class of 1969, spoke of his fond memories of life as a boarder at the college.

He recalled Fr Allen arriving as a new boy in Form 3 and how this warm and engaging character was quickly accepted into a well-established friendship group.

Mr Murphy said that in his travels across Gippsland he often spoke with people who had encountered Fr Allen and observed that he left each parish in which he served a richer place.

Catholic College Sale board member and 1970 student, Paul McDonough, recalled playing in the college football team with Fr Allen.

Following his ordination, Fr Allen returned to Sale and the young priest was highly regarded throughout the community.

Paul McAninly, college captain in 1970, read greetings to Fr Allen from the many Old Boys from across the state, from interstate and overseas who were unable to attend.

Many generous donations had been received and a presentation was made to Fr Allen.

Ray Linton of Sacred Heart Parish Morwell spoke of the fond memories the parishioners had of Fr Allen during his time as their parish priest.

Fr Allen recalled how, on arrival as a new boarder at St Pat's with his mother, the late Br Crispin met them.

Mrs Allen introduced her young son with "This is John Allen, Brother," to which Br Crispin replied, "No, he's Joffa Boy!" The nickname stuck!

Fr Allen spoke of each of the postings he has had in the diocese and noted that each parish had welcomed him in a special way, making each posting memorable to him.

A rousing rendition of For He's a Jolly Good Fellow was led by Gus Clifford.

A list of names of deceased classmates was prepared and presented to Fr Allen with the request that he offer a Mass for the repose of their souls.

- Catholic Life, October 2003.

Sermons linked the gospel and life

When delivering his sermons, Father John reached out to us in our own language and using relevant cultural images spoke about the gospels in a simple manner that we were all able to easily comprehend.

He was one of us.

As Peter Cahill wrote in his 2012 theology studies essay on John (further excerpts of which appear in the following chapter): "John maintains that his weekly homily is a cornerstone 'item' as pastoral leader of his parish. It is his once-per-week opportunity to 'feed' his parishioners and help them 'to connect Gospel and life' (his words). John's weekly routine, in preparing, is to read the Sunday scriptures (for the next week) each Monday, mulling over them and using them as a source of prayer. He would then explore the ideas of scripture scholars and commentaries on each reading. He would then seek out opportunities to make the readings connect to people's lives, especially in the context where they are living or working. In delivering his homily, he often moves from beyond the lectern in order to be closer to his listeners. He speaks with a mixture of wit, enthusiasm, sincerity and a sense of familiarity about Jesus whom he invariably places at the centre of his message. And he never speaks for more than 10 minutes!"

While at Narre Warren Father John gave sacraments program co-ordinator Emily D'Sylva the notes to some of his sermons to help her in her work in preparing children and adults for the sacraments. She kindly consented to share them with us. These are skeleton notes, with John adding other thoughts and injecting his own brand of humour as the sermon would unfold. They give us quite some insight into the man that was Father John.

They were delivered well before John was diagnosed with cancer. Yet the first one in particular demonstrates that death held no fear for him. He was prepared to meet his maker.

Where your treasure is, your heart will be also

Last week the gospel told the story about the man with the bumper wheat crop and warned against storing up riches, rather than striving to be rich in the sight of God. This Sunday the same theme continues:

"Get yourself a purse that will not wear out, treasure that will not fail you - where your treasure is, there your heart will be also."

Or, the chilling reminder, "You must stand ready, because the Son of Man is coming at an hour you do not expect." We must always be prepared.

Father Paul Newell, headmaster of Ampleforth College was attending a headmaster's conference in 1930. Another headmaster of a church school was rattling on about what his school tried to achieve. "What we must do," he said, "is to equip our boys for life."

Father Newell remarked out loud, "How interesting. At our school we always seek to prepare our boys for death."

Not as bad as it sounds. If you prepare for death then you are taking part in the best preparation for life. You are reflecting upon what is important in life, what life is giving you and what is important.

'Tuesdays with Morrie' is a novel by Mitch Albom, a sports writer from Detroit, that tells the story of an old professor named Morrie Schwartz and the huge influence he had on Albom as a 17-year-old boy. He discovers via the television show 'Nightline' that his mentor is dying of motor neuron disease and because he is able, he drives 700 kilometres to visit him one Tuesday. He will visit him 14 Tuesdays more before Morrie dies. As the relationship grows and develops, Albom's character changes as Schwartz's stories inspire him. He gains much from the interaction.

The only things that Albom brings to the old man in his suffering are food and company. They talk acceptance, communication, love, values, openness and happiness, coming to the conclusion that we must "love each other or perish."

When the old man has only 24 hours to live he organizes a funeral party for himself. He gets up early and goes for a swim and a walk in the garden, eats a big breakfast, works at his desk, lunches with a friend, has another walk in the park, enjoys dinner with his family and then is set for a contented, good night's sleep.

Morrie stood ready for the coming of the Son of Man. He was prepared. He was prepared because his treasure was laid in a place, deep inside himself where no thief could reach it. By learning how to die, he had learnt how to live. Fully, one day at a time, always ready.

Hypocrisy and sin

Father John was loved because he possessed humility and a humanity that we all identified with. He did not sit in judgment; he was one of us and accepted us as we were. In this sermon he talks about the hypocrisy of religious and the religions.

In 1989 Iran's Ayatollah Khomeini called for the execution of the Indian novelist Salman Rushdie whose novel 'The Satanic Verses' was denounced as blasphemous.

Although many people thought that the novel was in bad taste because it deeply offended the Muslim faith, the Western world was horrified at Khomeini's stance.

When 'The Last Temptation of Christ', Martin Scorsese's film, opened in Paris the year before, irate Christians burned down the cinema.

In July 2001 a man walked into the reception area of a Melbourne abortion clinic and shot a security guard dead.

In Rome, not more than a stone's throw from the Vatican, there is a statue to Giordano Bruno, a great Dominican philosopher. This man was burned alive at this exact spot in the 17th century, sentenced to death by Pope Clement VIII for being a heretic. Bruno was an unorthodox thinker who offended the then current Christian thinking. Today he is regarded as the father of modern western philosophy and thought.

All these people I have told you about - the Ayatollah, Clement VIII, orthodox Christians, the Pharisees and the Scribes - held uncompromising views of religion, mostly interested in maintaining their own world view and being unable or unwilling to examine it in any other way.

If we are truthful to ourselves, that form of hypocrisy exists in us all. Although most of us contend that we can't stand hypocrites, if we look into our souls we will probably find hypocrisy there.

We rail against the trash found written and shown about Lara Bingle and Michael Clarke in the media but most of us read it and enjoy it – on the quiet.

We take great pleasure in spotting a phoney but fail to see the phoniness within ourselves.

Perhaps we are only being honest when we point out the faults of others, but then we become outraged when somebody points to our faults.

How much time do we spend gossiping? It is a fact of life that most people who readily condemn others are trying to hide their own guilt.

We try to detract from our own sins by decrying others. Rather we should recognize that it is good to come out and acknowledge our own weaknesses. The Catholic Church should do this as well, admit our own struggle, our lack of perfection.

Paul tells us that we all share a common humanity. This is interesting as he is telling us that everything is meant for good, even sin.

Once we confront sin in ourselves there is no room for hypocrisy anymore, no room for judgment of others. Sin can free us to be kind, to be merciful, to be humble.

Losers become winners – Luke's Gospels

It is a story we know so well as we have heard it so many times. Perhaps if we look at it in another light we might transcend its familiarity.

This story is the last episode in what we might call 'Luke's Loser Cycle'. I say this because one after another he presents us with losses – the lost statue, the lost coin, the lost sheep and today the lost son.

The 'loser status' came quickly when Jesus let a woman of the street touch him, wash his feet and then dry them with her hair. His host was appalled. This man had invited Jesus into his home thinking he was a prophet, somebody worth knowing. He was filled with disgust when he witnessed Jesus touch a fallen woman and there and then vowed never to invite him again or have anything to do with him. In his eyes, by doing these things, Jesus had lost his status as a prophet.

We already knew because the Gospel told us, that Jesus ate with the enemy, the tax collectors and the sinners, the corrupt and a Roman offsider. By mixing with what was considered low life, he lost his status with his peers.

In Luke's Gospels many things were lost. Jesus lost his status, a housewife lost her coin, a farmer his sheep and now in today's story the father has lost his son. There are losses everywhere.

What is Luke trying to tell us?

Sometimes, out of a fool's mouth comes wisdom. The owner of the NBC, Ted Turner, who is also one of the most bigoted men in America said, "Christianity is for losers". He didn't mean it as a compliment. He thought it was an insult. But we Christians think it is good news.

Christianity is for losers.

It is for those who have lost virtue, hope, pride, position, wealth, health and life.

It is for those who have lost everything, but in losing, have found themselves and because of this their eyes are open to God's tender mercy.

Let me tell you a famous losing story about a man called Steven Cook. Steven Cook told a terrible lie, which caused another person terrible, shocking pain.

He claimed that when he was a seminarian in Chicago his professor had sexually abused him. As if that was not terrible enough, this professor was now the Archbishop of Chicago, a man named Cardinal Joseph Bernardin. The story made headlines around the world. The cardinal was humiliated and lost his status and his good name.

Eight months after the initial accusation, Steven Cook retracted his statement and admitted that he was lying.

The cardinal did not gloat. Instead, like in the story of the prodigal son, he took the initiative and arranged a meeting with his false accuser. He reached out to meet his wayward son.

Cook apologized in a simple and direct way, asking for forgiveness. He received the reconciliation he sought but then Bernardin offered to celebrate Mass there and then. Cook was reluctant as he was alienated from the church. The cardinal did not push him but opened his briefcase and took out a chalice and a Bible that somebody had given him.

"What do you say, Steven?" he asked.

Steven broke down and asked to participate. The prodigal winner had become a loser because of the love of his spiritual father.

This is a story but it is also our story.

God is Love all embracing.

He waits and does not give up.

He wants to reconcile the world.

He wants us to come home to him.

40 days in the desert

I read something this week that really struck a chord with me. It was too late to be shared on Ash Wednesday so I'll share it with you now.

Since last Lent many things that were once alive in us have probably died and turned to ash. Love and loved ones have died, illness has struck, friendships may have been broken. Illusions about others or ourselves may have been destroyed. It is out of such ashes that we hope Christians will rise up to new life.

In the season of Lent the church calls us back to traditional Christian practice, to prayer, fasting and action.

The Japanese have a beautiful proverb that says, "Something of the fragrance of the flower lingers on the hands of the giver."

When we give we also receive.

Whatever we do in Lent should seep unobtrusively into our world and our relationships.

The gift will transform us with the "lingering fragrance that comes from knowing Him."

"And my speech and my message were not in plausible words of wisdom, but in demonstration of the Spirit and of power." (1 Corinthians, 2:4.)

Lent has begun and we are called into the desert, a place where many saints and mystics went to find themselves. It is a lonely place.

Priest and writer Henri Nouwen once said, "A life without a lonely place that is a quiet centre, can easily become destructive."

We need to take time and space to reflect. We need to go to our personal desert.

So what happens in the desert? It seems that nothing happens and yet, if we look closely, on closer scrutiny there are many things going on. The desert is an ever changing and growing place.

In Lent we should take ourselves to our personal desert, our quiet place, and ask ourselves these questions: "What happens in my heart? In what do I believe?"

In the Arthur Miller play, 'Death of a Salesman' the central character Willy Loman is a tragic figure. His life of self-destruction tragically ends in suicide, very sad, and Willy's son makes this statement about his father that says it all: "He never knew who he was."

Please know who you are. Take time to reflect on this in Lent. "Who am I? Why am I here?"

Before he began his public ministry Jesus was led by the spirit out into the desert where he was tempted.

The temptation of Jesus always reminds me of Homer's epic poem, 'The Odyssey', which tells the story of Odysseus' voyage home to Ithaca following the fall of Troy. It was a hazardous journey, a road of trials, and he was forced to endure many obstacles. In order to get home he must pass the Island of the Siren, where a sea nymph lived. She had the head of a beautiful woman and the body of a bird. The songs she sang were so sweet and enticing that they lured sailors to destruction on the rocks below. Odysseus is aware of her charms and plans for the onslaught so that he can defeat the siren. He blocks his ears with wax so that he cannot hear her song.

However, he is tempted and gives into temptation because he wishes to hear the seductive voice just once! In order to do that but still avoid being drawn to the island, he lashes himself with rope to the mast of the boat.

The siren represents all the things that may be alluring in life but which may lead us to destruction. How do we avoid the dangers of sin?

Jesus goes into the desert so that he can reflect and ask himself the questions: "What does it mean to be the anointed one? What is the true mission God is calling me to do?"

These are the same two questions we all must answer: "Who am I? What am I called to do?"

That reminds me of the story about the eagle who was brought up in the chicken pen. One day he looks towards the sky and asks, "What is that creature soaring high above us, seeing the world?"

"That is an eagle," his chicken mother replies.

"Am I an eagle?" asks the eagle of his chicken mother.

"No, my dear, you are a chicken, that bird is an eagle."

So the poor eagle thought he was a chicken and so was doomed to live and die like a chicken, never soaring in the sky, but always scratching in the ground for worms.

How many of us fail to discover the real eagle within ourselves and so spend our lives scratching.

RAINBOW OVER NARRE WARREN

A boy after four girls!
John, about eight months old, sitting up in the twin pram at the back of
the Orme Street home.
With him are Margaret (back), Kathleen, Joan and Elsie.

John, about three years old, with his first 'girlfriend' Maree Harris whose family was one of Carmel Holiday Flats' first clients. The Harris clan visited Lakes Entrance annually for many years and became firm friends.

The Allen family, circa 1965. John is in the centre and was about 13. He had just started at St Pat's College at Sale and is in his school uniform.
Back, from left: Arthur, Elsie, Kathleen, John, Margaret, Joan, Maureen.
Front: Theresa, Mary, Jack, Eileen.
Robert was born in 1966 and can be seen on the left. He was added later.

This is the last photograph taken of all 10 Allen siblings, in front of the family home in 2010.
Back, from left: Joan, Kathleen, John, Arthur, Mary, Robert.
Front: Margaret, Elsie, Maureen, Eileen.

Pretty girls were a mystery to the boarding school boys! John, aged about 16, at a St Pat's/Our Lady of Sion dance. Neither of them seem too sure of themselves!

John, aged 19, with his sister Joan on her wedding day in June 1971.

John with his mother Theresa in his first year studying to be a priest at Corpus Christi College, Werribee.

Which one is the priest? John with brothers-in-law Ross Keeley (left) and Graeme Johnstone on the beach at Broome, WA, in 1991.

John in St Pat's cricket cap with his father Jack, left, and brother-in-law Ross at a match at the WACA, Perth, in the 1980s.

John loved his family and shared many happy times with them. He was included in everybody's special celebrations and always made an effort to attend. He especially loved his nieces and nephews, and they in turn loved and appreciated him.

Left: With niece Erin Santamaria at the Ninety Mile Beach at Lakes Entrance.

Above: John loved to swim. Here he is with sisters Maureen, Elsie and Joan and brother-in-law David at Lakes Entrance in the early 1980s.

Left: In 1987 with nephew Chris Johnstone on the occasion of his Confirmation.

At a gathering with the Paparo, Ross, Keeley and Santamaria families at the Johnstone's home in the early 1990s. John is in the back row, centre.

Officiating as Jack and Theresa renew their vows on the occasion of their 50th wedding anniversary in 1996.

John had a lovely relationship with all of his nieces and nephews. He always gave them time, let them tease him and have fun with him.
Above: With niece Lynda (Morrison) Capes, her husband Michael and daughter Sophie.
Below: With niece Therese (Keeley) Brooks.

Picnicking with Ross, Therese and Mary Keeley, and Tessa and Eloise Johnstone.

It is always party time in a big extended family and John enjoyed them all.

With Maureen and Erin Santamaria.

Hamming it up with brother-in-law Laurie Appleby.

Also, consider how many of us spend our lives doing things that seem to be important but are in fact, utterly futile?

I leave you with this thought.

The other day, I was watering the plants when I saw my neighbour sprinkling breadcrumbs around his front garden.

"Are you feeding the birds?" I asked.

I was surprised at his answer.

"No," he said, "I am sprinkling bread to keep the tigers away from my garden."

"But there aren't any tigers for thousands of miles," I replied.

He smiled a smile of contentment.

"Yes, it's very effective, isn't it?"

The Crucifixion

Two years ago I visited the Church of the Holy Sepulchre in Jerusalem. It is considered to be the site where Jesus was crucified, buried and rose from the dead. I found it a wonderfully prayerful and simple place to visit and a place where I could take time to stop and reflect. However, there is another side to this church.

It is like so many places in Jerusalem because it is constantly being fought over. Much blood has been shed in its name. This weekend, with both the Eastern and Western churches celebrating Easter at the same time, there is bound to be a 'rumble in the jungle'.

It is not so much the Catholic tradition, but more the Eastern Orthodox churches who, over time, have had to pitch battles over disputed lands and demanding justice for displaced peoples. For most Christians, including myself, these battles are a source of great scandal.

My visit to Jerusalem has caused me to ponder about what makes people who should be united become continually divided and at war with each other. It is something that happens so much in life.

Too often we see this division happen, even within our own families. For example, a person who has been a forceful and unifying person dies and this moment in time - which should be a time to celebrate, reflect and remember - instead becomes a battleground. Families are torn apart by a fight over the will, what should happen at the funeral service and all of those other earthly conflicts that distract them from the real reason they are together.

The death of Jesus Christ was no different. Here was a young man who died violently and innocently, leaving an incredible gap in the lives of so many people. They were sad and lonely without him. The disciples scattered.

Only John, Mary and the women disciples remained.

Thomas denies Jesus.

Peter disowns him.

Judas betrays him.

The list of treachery goes on and on.

The death of Jesus is an event that triggers major traumas, unanswered questions, loneliness and doubt for those who have loved and surrounded him. It is no different today.

A violent death of anybody before his/her time turns our world upside down and inside out.

That is the reason why, today, we don't celebrate the death of Jesus, we remember him with love.

With hindsight, we are lucky because we know the story. We know that Jesus will rise on the third day and will vindicate his awful, violent death. If Jesus did not rise from the dead, his death would have been a pure blasphemy. But he did!

Our belief in Jesus is important. We must know who this man is, and what his mission in life was all about.

When we say the Son of God, we embrace all aspects in our lives except sin. He represents the fullness and truth of life.

This all flows so easily off our tongues but what exactly do we mean?

Who is this man on the cross with his hands outstretched?

He is embracing us all with his love and embracing the world with all of our struggles, joy and pain. God is suffering with us!

Let me tell you a story:

Chaim Potok, a Jewish Rabbi, is an author who wrote one of my favourite books, 'My Name is Asher Lev'. It is about a community of Hasidic Jews known as 'Ladovers Caffe' after the town of Ladov in Russia where their founder was born. It is a very orthodox movement who are filled with a great love and observance of the Torah.

It is the story of a young Jewish boy whose art causes conflict with his family and other members of his community. The boy, Asher, possesses a great love of painting but lives in a community where art is not highly regarded, or even regarded at all. This Jewish community considers art is unrelated to religious expression and at best is a waste of time and, at worst, is possibly a sacrilege.

The book follows Asher's maturity as both an artist and a Jew.

His father rejects his son's art as foolishness, telling him that this talent of his comes from the dark side. The boy listens but is not deterred.

His mother understands better and supports his gift but is torn between what her husband wants and what her son wishes to do. However, they are lucky to have a wise Rabbi who is open to Asher's gift. He encourages an expert artist to mentor Asher Lev and take him under his wing.

Eventually Asher becomes an accomplished artist, but this does not change his father's view. The father stands firm to his convictions and says, "He has betrayed me."

The story finally reaches a crisis point when Asher tries to depict the anguish of his mother in a painting. He shows her as she is, torn between her two loves - her husband and her son. To depict the anguish of his mother, he borrows the image of the Christian faith, the Crucifixion.

Picasso, the great artist, has famously said, "Great art is a lie which makes us realize the truth."

This is exactly what the Jewish boy does. He tells a lie to depict the truth and his work quickly becomes a masterpiece. It is called 'Brooklyn Crucifixion'.

In it the mother is crucified and the father and son stand together at the foot of the cross. We see the conflict between tradition and individualism, religion and art. It is constant and lifelong. The father is painted as bewildered, angry and sad.

Because of this painting, Asher cops it from both sides - from the Jews because they consider he has wasted his time on the frivolous and from the Christians because they consider his painting a blasphemous mockery.

And why do you think he chose this Christian image?

Probably because he could think of no image from his own faith that portrayed a mother's lonely torment, agony, anguish and suffering. He was drawn to the image of the crucified one.

The anguish and suffering of the crucified one is the anguish of God who loved the world so much that he accepted torment, ridicule and death.

We, as people of faith, see more than that. We see it as a sign of love and hope for a suffering world.

The Easter story

The story of Easter moves from darkness to light, from grieving to believing. Mary Magdalene is a person who has experienced the darkness of death.

We are told specifically that she came to the tomb while it is still dark because she is distraught that Jesus is dead.

The darkness is all around her - her grief, pain, loss and the realization of the finality of death.

She goes to the tomb, not to anoint or for any other reason. She goes simply because she needs to be there, close to Jesus whom she loved. At that time there is nowhere else she wants to be. Mary Magdalene loved him so she wanted to be near him. Even in death.

Mary Magdalene represents the darkness that surrounds all of our lives at some time - the darkness of pain, sickness, death, brokenness, violence.

At this moment our own church is surrounded by the pain of broken trust, the darkness experienced by the victims of sexual abuse by our clergy. The misguided and closed response of the church appears to many as a cover up. The whole unholy mess causes all of us so much pain and darkness.

But let us not dwell there. It is quite appropriate that the Easter story began in darkness, but then something unexpected happened.

When Mary got to the tomb the stone that sealed the entrance had been moved. She is unable to comprehend and she cries out in distress, "They have taken my Lord!"

When Peter sees the empty cloth in which Jesus had been wrapped he knows that the body has not been stolen. The beloved disciple sees and believes. He knows that Christ has risen!

The story concludes, "They did not understand the scripture that he had to rise from death."

Why did Jesus rise from the dead?

God will not allow death to be victorious.

God is not absent even in our darkest times.

God will not allow death to have the last word.

Now, the Hopi Indians live in Arizona.

Children there undergo an interesting initiation rite at an early age that centres upon masked spirits named Kachina who visit the village in order to terrify the children. It is a ceremony that is deliberately pointed towards bringing about a process of disenchantment that will mark the children's entry into adulthood.

The Kachina visit, they tell scary stories, and after they have frightened the children witless, they perform a dance for them.

In the final part of the ceremony, the children are taken to a dark, ceremonial cave for the last dance. Anxiety reigns. The children don't know what to expect. They are petrified.

Then the Kachina throw off their masks and the children discover that they are not evil spirits but they are their neighbours in masks!

Hopi Indians believe that although the children suffer disenchantment and bewilderment in this initiation, it introduces them to the natural way of life, leads them to adulthood and helps them to let go of childhood.

We are the same. If, at first the experience of disenchantment appears to be cruel and negative, shattering our world, all is not lost. We should look at it as an opportunity to rethink and to discover the truth at a deeper level.

To return to the state of our church for a moment.

These dark days will hopefully help us to discover our faith at a deeper level. More people will be called to take more responsibility for the church and we must realize that all of us are called, not just we priests. Together we can make a difference.

Let us take this painful experience that we are going through, and like Mary Magdalene, may we pray that our feelings of loss and disappointment will morph into the discovery and joy of the resurrection.

On vocations to the priesthood

The other day I was reading an article about the shortage of vocations to the priesthood, diaconate and the religious life.

The writer was saying that the shortage must be seen in the larger context of vocations in general.

That is to say, lots of secular vocations are struggling to attract people - nursing, teaching, medicine, social work.

The vocations crisis, in other words, is part of a wider social issue that reveals the heart of modern society.

What has happened is that an external marketplace mentality has replaced the sense of an internal calling to better society.

For example, the article quoted a report about nursing that says, "Nursing's collapse is a cultural and spiritual one, a failure of the notion of charity and compassion, not a result of failed pay bargaining."

In other words our world today places emphasis primarily on attending the right school in order to make the right connections in order to land the big jobs that go with the big money.

A vocational culture, on the other hand, is one in that people have a sense of being called to make life better, a sense of possessing a gift, a sense that they can live a worthwhile life and do things that count on a human level whether or not it brings money or fame.

This sense of vocation is at the opposite end of what society views as success; the opposite side of prestige and power, what we can buy and sell.

We pay the Qantas boss $10 million to move jobs offshore so that he can appear successful.

We pay a footballer $1 million while we give a carer for the elderly $15 per hour.

Big money does not equate with inner peace.

Many of us are not satisfied. When we reach the top, so many of us are filled with an emptiness that comes with the lack of the four "c's" in our lives - care, compassion, charity and a cause. These things are larger than we are.

Most people are good and do look for something that is greater than ourselves.

If we think about it, perhaps what is lacking in our educational system is this sense of us all being human and that we are all on this earth together. What we do does make a difference.

Father John – a case study

As part of his Graduate Diploma in Theology studies in 2012, Peter Cahill of Berwick interviewed John for a case study, 'Father John Allen, Parish Priest of Our Lady Help of Christians Narre Warren, February 1994 – June 2011: an exemplar of parish leadership'.

This essay explored, in some detail, Father John's tenure and its many achievements at Narre Warren.

Here are some excerpts that describe the man and his work:

Father John Allen, a priest of the Sale diocese, was ordained in 1978. In 1994, he began his tenure at Our Lady Help of Christians Parish at Narre Warren, a large and continually expanding parish. He remained there until mid-2011 and left a highly impressive legacy as parish leader. Indeed, this parish is regarded as something of the 'jewel in the crown' in the Sale diocese. John's success was based on a combination of well-nurtured inner spiritually, an inner confidence, a capacity to delegate and trust others, enthusiasm and a realistic optimism. He also possesses outstanding 'people skills'.

Of the priests who serve the church and its people, there are many, it needs to be said, who do so with both joy and undoubted competence. In this short case study, I discuss a contemporary priest who, in both lifestyle and achievements, epitomizes many of the ideals outlined in the Vatican documents. To all who observe him and work with him, he appears totally at ease with his role and rejoices in it. He is, indeed, an exemplary parish priest and fine leader of his flock.

The Narre Warren parish is situated at the extreme western end of the Sale diocese that runs from Narre Warren to the New South Wales border. Narre Warren lies at the centre of an area whose population expansion has been among the quickest in Australia's urban history. Literally, hundreds of people move into the suburbs of Narre Warren, Cranbourne, Berwick and Pakenham on a weekly basis. John informs me that the Narre Warren parish is now the second largest in Australia and boasts of a large (but often insufficiently large) church, and three primary schools. A total of 20,000 Catholics are listed as members of the parish, with 3000 attending Mass each weekend.

The ethnic mix of the parish has changed markedly from predominantly Anglo-Saxon populace of 25 years ago. There is a significant Asian presence, with the Philippines, India and Sri Lanka being the dominant groupings. The parish also provides students to St Francis Xavier College, a three-campus co-educational Catholic secondary college. Whilst some of the parish and area expansion began prior to John's arrival at Narre Warren, the tsunami-like explosion of people coincided very much with his time there.

When I asked John what vision he had for his new parish when he arrived, he claimed that he had none. He believed that it would be presumptuous to set out a vision until he had a firm sense of the nature and dynamics of this parish. As a starting point, he first wanted to speak with parishioners, to ascertain their needs and wishes. Some of his first initiatives were: appointing a finance committee to address the issue of the parish debt ensuring that all committee members were either accountants or bank managers; expanding the office staff, nearly all of whom were chosen or elected by members of the parish (he informed me that he eschewed appointing anyone like himself as he did not want people 'just like me'); the establishment of an expanded Parish Pastoral Council, elected by the parishioners of Narre Warren; the appointment of a business manager and a Sacramental co-ordinator.

John also addressed the issue of a bigger church. The key issue was to choose between building an entirely new structure or expanding and refurbishing the existing church. After many parish meetings and canvassing people's views thoroughly, the latter option was chosen.

Whilst all this was happening, John was getting acquainted with his parishioners and they him. He placed a strong emphasis on home visitations - to the sick, to new arrivals to the parish, to young couples preparing for their child's Baptism, and to the 'ordinary' parish member whom he believed warranted a visit from their new pastor. He also developed or encouraged/initiated choirs and liturgical groups in order to ensure a meaningful liturgical service at all four Eucharistic celebrations each weekend.

As his parish expanded further, John continued to innovate, create, consult and connect. Always a relaxed communicator and possessed of very sound people skills, he claims that it was during this period that he really learned to trust. As parish leader, he had, in the past, kept a too-watchful eye (and hand) on events in the parish. He began to realize that not only was this now physically impossible, but it was unnecessary. A plethora of parish groups emerged, some due to his direct initiative but many of these due to the fact that parishioners felt encouraged to develop these groups under the guidance and with the blessing of their pastor. This required judgment on his part, and a genuine belief that the Spirit was at work amongst his parishioners.

Some further significant developments during these years were: the appointment of a permanent deacon and, later, the appointment of a second priest; the building of a state-of-the-art sound system for the church, thus enhancing greatly liturgical experiences for the always-growing congregations; a complete refurbishment and expansion of the church; establishing a third primary school; the appointment of a dynamic and passionate Josephite sister as pastoral associate. John had worked with Sister Doreen in a previous context and the two of them exhibited an outstanding and very effective working relationship. The mission of Jesus flowered at Narre Warren because the giftedness of so many was recognized and bore fruit.

When reflecting on his sixteen-and-a-half years at Narre Warren, John feels mainly joy, as well as a wonderful sense of achievement. When pressed on those aspects of leadership that he strove to develop, he nominates seven key themes or elements:

(a) As spiritual leader, an acute awareness of the need for daily prayer.

(b) The importance of a spiritual director who acted as mentor and adviser. He meets regularly with a religious sister and regards these meetings as essential.

(c) Trusting, not controlling, those in his parish who are responsible for a myriad of parish activities.

(d) An ability to listen.

(e) A real joy in working with others developing a series of teams within the parish.

(f) A capacity and willingness to offer positive feedback on a regular basis.

(g) Optimism, but always with a realistic edge.

There was certainly 'true dignity' and both 'compassion' and 'inclusion' about Father John Allen. These latter qualities were two of the more pronounced traits during his Narre Warren years where he enjoyed the constant and varied chance for 'interaction with others in organizational life'. Such interactions energise, provoke ideas and provide genuine chances for growth. John takes seriously the life of Jesus as inspiration and leadership model. The image of Jesus he regularly presents is one which stresses love over an addiction to rules and a call to be counter-cultural in living out one's Christian faith. He calls his parishioners to look out for ways to alleviate the suffering of others, and to work creatively and compassionately to redress society's ills. In living out his role of parish priest, John always presented an image of one who was called to serve, in the same way as Jesus, did, and who was profoundly comfortable in this role. At the same time, there was never a doubt in people's minds as to who was the parish leader.

I believe that at Narre Warren parishioners feel empowered and the sense of partnership between pastor and parishioners is palpable. One of the ongoing benefits of this empowerment of parishioners is that it allows a parish to continue to thrive long after the parish priest has departed. This is a further and admirable legacy of John Allen's outstanding tenure at this parish.

Narre Warren farewells Father John

I knew that my brother, John was a good priest who did his job diligently and well.

Whenever I had been to Mass in Narre Warren I was always impressed by the wonderful ambience of love and tolerance that emanated from the congregation. People were just happy to be there, praying together and forming community.

I had been to the openings of two primary schools where community was being created from a paddock on the outskirts of the developing suburb. I had been with John in Dandenong or in the city and it seemed that he knew everybody and everybody was pleased to say 'hello'.

But my husband Graeme and I were blown away by the outpouring of love and affection on the day that Narre Warren sent him off to a new parish after 16 years when he walked amongst them. It was amazing!

Father John's last day at Narre Warren in January 2011 was a wonderful combination of joy and tears, laughter and sadness, memories and prayer. It underlined how the parish had grown, what it had achieved and the tremendous sense of community that had flourished under his leadership. They presented Father John with an astonishing array of gifts, including Essendon memorabilia and a huge Bomber teddy bear. As well, John was given the perfect set-up for a man who loves his sport – a massive recliner, which became known as 'Big Chair', a huge flat-screen television and a brand new comfy bed.

How wonderful that his loved parishioners had the opportunity to show him before he became ill that he was truly loved. John used those gifts as the perfect reference point for his emotion-charged farewell speech. Below is an edited transcript.

"Wherever I go, it will be different – it won't be the same."

I was overwhelmed when I was told what gifts you were giving me as a parish. You know how you regress back to your childhood? Well I think with all this I will be regressing back! Because when I was growing up, Mum used to accuse me during the cricket season of rotating from the bed to the couch to the television, and back to bed again. So as I go into middle age - or late age! - I will be able to do exactly that every summer, won't I? Sit up in my seat, watch the television, and then roll in to bed. And that is what my idea of a life fulfilled will be.

So, thank you so much for everything. For your generosity and for organizing today, to everybody involved in the parish pastoral council.

This is also a chance, although I have already spoken in church, to say some thank-you's to people.

First of all, thank you to all of the parish. It is a wonderful parish we live in here, and that's one of the great sadnesses about leaving. Because, wherever I go, it will be different, it won't be the same, and I will miss all the people of Narre Warren. That's the reality of it. It has been a marvellous 16 years here.

So I simply say to everybody, "Thank you". Because your spirit, your openness, your ownership of the parish, your sense of involvement and your general experience of life just enriches the parish so much. Above all, your strong faith! I think that is the wonderful thing about dealing with people from a multicultural background. The strength of faith that you bring; your lives and faith are so totally intertwined.

Now, turning to some people I must individually thank today. First of all, to Father Matthew, I wish him all the best. As I said this morning at the eight o'clock Mass, he is probably one of the better fellows I have lived with over my time as a priest. He is so easy to get along with, he is so adaptable, he is good fun, he works hard and he is a marvellous fellow all around. So I wish him all the best. Thank you to him for the three years I have had with him.

Thank you to John and the Pastoral Council for organizing today. We've got a great pastoral council, an excellent council running the parish. So, thank you, John, to everybody.

To Paul and John representing our schools. We have got marvellous schools in the parish and great leadership and I am grateful for all that you do on behalf of the church in Narre Warren, Berwick and in this region.

Now, to some people who have worked with me - I think it is important to acknowledge them. First, Maureen who was my housekeeper, and has been for about 12 years.

Thank you, Maureen. Everybody should know that she does such a good job. You know that whatever is said in the house it never ever goes outside those four walls. She is gentle and she is adaptable. Thanks to her and also to Phyllis, who helps her often, and to Eugene over the years.

To Suzie, who has been parish secretary for close on 11 years now. When Suzie was appointed I remember thinking, "Well, here we've got someone who is really going to be marvellous."

And she has been. Suzie is dependable, she is capable and she sees it as her parish. She has got ownership of the parish and she has done a marvellous job. So Suzie, thank you. And also to Phillip and the family.

To Colleen, too, and Lex and the family. Colleen, of course, works with Suzie and does a mighty job. We are very fortunate to have two very, very capable secretaries. So Colleen and Suzie, thank you.

Richard, our business manager. I hate dealing with books and finance! And I remember one day Richard arrived at the front door and said, "Look, my wife has sent me down. She wants me to do something in the parish. I'm getting in the way at home!"

I said to him, "What do you do?" and he said, "Well, I was a bank manager."

And I thought, "I know where I can put you to work!"

He has done a marvellous job since. So Richard thank you, too. And to all the other helpers in the office. To Carmel and Jocelyn who help out and so many others who come and go and help at different times, as well.

I would like to mention Louisa, who worked with me so long up until this year and has moved to Sydney. Also, I would like to remember a couple of people who have died in my time and have worked with me; two people who worked in our parish office as staff - Veronica, of course, Veronica Scammell, who was our sacramental coordinator for so long. She was probably the most organized person I ever knew. If Veronica told me to do something, I did it, I tell you. And it was done; it was always very well organized. Veronica got sick when she was very, very young - I know Michael is here today with some of the children - but Veronica was an exceptional person.

And the other one - and I know Andrea is here somewhere today - was Mary Lees who worked in the office, probably our first parish worker. Mary, of course, was the quiet, gentle English lady from Manchester, with a beautiful manner. Mary died in her early forties, too. Again, very, very young. Just to acknowledge them today and the families and the great work they have done over the years.

And also Kath Ornsby who worked with me when I was first here.

Now of course, there are others, too. There is Trevor Scott, our maintenance man. And Malcolm Gore. It's one month today since Malcolm passed away. They are volunteers around the parish but work more or less fulltime and I am very grateful for that too.

Trevor and I often go to the football together, too - we share a common interest. But he's not getting the Bomber teddy bear, I can tell you! He'll have to fight me for it.

And of course, my pastoral workers - Doreen, who has organized today, and I know that. The good fun and joy that Doreen brings to the parish, and a real sense of vitality. I mean, there are always lots of things done at the last minute, but they get done!

It's marvellous the way Doreen works. She has a great gift with people, particularly with people who have just arrived from overseas. They have probably never, ever met a religious nun like Sister Doreen ever in their life. Whether you are from India, Pakistan or Indonesia you are probably thinking, "What have we struck here?" When she comes up and says "I'm Sister Doreen," you can see their eyes just about popping out. But she does a marvellous job. She brings people together, with great energy and fun.

Also to remember Aileen, who worked here for a number of years at the parish. She is not very well at the moment, but Aileen was a lady who really cared for the battlers. She did a marvellous job.

The Good Shepherd sisters, too. They have been with me for about 16 years and were a wonderful support. Of course, dear Sister Elizabeth died just six weeks ago. I remember her, too, and Margaret and Adrienne.

Deacon Peter! One of the great gifts to the parish. He arrived a few years ago and said he would like to work with us and I asked what he would like to do and he said, "Well, I would like to get involved with ministering to the sick."

And that was probably one of the most neglected ministries in our parish. So I said, "Just go for it." And he has! He has organized it and he got people around him. He's got a hundred volunteers and every sick person in our parish is cared for, every nursing home is taken care of.

It's been marvellous co-operation - Peter is a good listener and works, I suppose, in the way I would like to work but I sometimes don't. He enables people to do things. Peter, you have been a great support and friend too, and I say thank you.

Then there is Rosemary, of course. Rosemary's not here today. She went and had a big two-month holiday to the United Kingdom. What a great time to go - she has been frozen in ever since!

Rosemary has got marvellous knowledge, a love of the church, and she is really good with people. She looks after the RCIA and different areas like that. So it's important we acknowledge that. You see, I don't mean to differentiate, just to highlight people, to acknowledge the people I have worked closely with.

Joe, our Sacristan, thank you. He's progressed from being the Bishop of Narre Warren to being the Sacristan of Narre Warren. Every parish needs at least one Joe! If you get two, it's good. Joe is just marvellous. I roll over here at ten to eight to say Mass every Sunday and everything is set up. You come over every day and everything is set up. He cleans up afterwards, and it's all done in a voluntary capacity. So, Joe, thank you. He does a great job.

Down the back there is John our security man. He's marvellous, too, locking up, setting things up, doing a marvellous job. John's sister and my mum were great mates at Lakes Entrance, so there's another connection. And of course his brother-in-law is still good friends of our family. So, John, the work you do with security is marvellous and so is your generosity.

I think you know, my family are here today. A lot of them are here, some couldn't be here. My family gave me faith. Mum and Dad taught me that faith meant putting back into life. I hope I have been able to do that. They also taught me – I think especially Mum and Dad, the way in which they always welcomed people, their involvement in the parish, how their table was always open to people – to love people and to trust people. I think that is an important thing for anybody, but I think as a priest these days you have got to know that. If you don't trust people, community doesn't happen. I do try to trust people, although sometimes I might fall down in that area.

So it's just to say thank you today for everybody and everything; to say how much this parish has meant to me. It's been my life for sixteen-and-a-half years. It's been my life's work! In a sense I have created something here, which I know I am very proud of, because of you.

Of course, today I feel a bit sad about going but I also know it is the right thing. In some ways, I feel a real sense of peace with it, too. So I think that is a good decision.

Ah, you know, I would have liked to stay another year, and then a year after that. I probably would have liked to die here, but that might have been quicker than I expected.

But I have really enjoyed my time here. You have been a lovely group of people; I won't forget you. So take care.

Thank you for you generosity always and for what you have been to me in the last 16 years.

Shocking news, but John accepts it

After a well-earned sabbatical, John settled into his new parish of Iona/Maryknoll/Koo Wee Rup. But despite a trip savouring the sights and sounds of India, he was not feeling well and a visit to the doctor in December 2012 revealed the devastating cause - he had pancreatic cancer.

John began a journal but only made two entries, preferring to concentrate his time and energy on his treatment, contemplation, prayer and doing as many 'normal' things as he could.

The two entries he wrote give you some insight into how he quickly accepted his situation, even though he had no control over what was happening to him. These are his words:

08/01/2013

I started writing and reflecting today after visiting the oncologist – he was very direct and to the point, and after the flickering hope of last week he destroyed it in one minute. The word 'incurable', six to 14 months maybe. A sledgehammer hit me.

For the next four to five hours I sat like a block of ice - not feeling, thinking, doing, a surreal experience. It was like a curtain had opened on a whole new world and I was just a mere spectator.

Gail Ryan came and spent some time. It was lovely, got me talking again. Rob and Roger brought dinner, Maureen and David came, a lovely five hours. I have always known but in the last three to four weeks I have really experienced what a lovely caring family I have. They love me and I love them deeply. Saying goodbye until we meet again will be so hard.

Three things occurred to me.

- I am not afraid of dying. Death holds no fear and I firmly believe that in the end, life changes, it is not ended.

- I really fear the suffering that may lay ahead. I know it is something I can't control but the doctors assure me that it will be carefully monitored and controlled.

- How hard it is to live without planning too far ahead, having to let go of the things that give you comfort and purpose. Simply having to live in the present. With the help of God I can do that.

Even in all the turbulence of today I realize through all of this, that I am surrounded by so much love. I know the importance of my faith gifted to me by God and by my parents.

09/01/2013

A good day yesterday. Rob and Rog brought a meal. Maureen and I attended our first chemo session. Everyone is tired. Hoges and Denis called and Hoges stayed for dinner.

Feeling a little better, prayed for an hour – prayer was a little harder. It is like you are swimming along then you hit a cold patch and the realization that maybe life is closing down rapidly, yet I still maintain a high degree of hope.

Denis anointed me and brought me Communion, which meant so much to me. My prayer focus is trying to be here at this moment - not this time last year, or in six week's time which could be scary. Now I do feel a real sense of peace.

The Scripture I use, Antonio Cardinal Bacci, "Lord that I may see," says: "The restlessness and the intensity of living make us see things as different from what they are. But one day the veil of the temple will be rent asunder before our frightened eyes and eternal light will break upon us. Then we shall be blind no longer, but we shall see everything in the light of eternity. Let us place ourselves now in the state in which we should like to find ourselves at that moment. Let us consider ourselves and everything else in the light of eternity. Then our blindness will disappear. Since we shall see everything in God's way we shall direct all our thoughts and actions towards Him."

I am overwhelmed by people's goodness and by my family who have simply downed tools to be with me. My eyes have been opened to incredible goodness and love. My family and friends have been a great comfort today.

Illness sparks an outpouring of love

Slowly the news got out that Father John had incurable cancer and very quickly people who loved him rallied around - writing, phoning and visiting.

In his hometown Lakes Entrance and in his beloved Narre Warren, novenas were made to Australia's own saint, Mary MacKillop. Heaven was stormed but God wanted John home with Him.

Here are some snippets of notes from the hundreds of cards and letters that John received from friends and parishioners while he was sick and dying. It is just a sample of the outpouring of love, affirmation and support he enjoyed from all over the country. Names have been deleted so that the sender remains anonymous and generic language used where necessary to keep them private.

Dear Father John,

May hope and faith bring you peace at this time. You are in our thoughts and prayers as you fight the biggest battle of your life. May God bless you dear friend.

Dear John,

Praying very specially for you at this difficult juncture in your life. May God give you the strength and courage to face each day and to cope with all the treatments required for your recovery. With much love.

We are holding you in our thoughts and prayers. You have always been a true friend.

Our dearest Father John,

We remember you in our thoughts and prayers. We love you and are grateful for all you have done for us. We know that miracles can happen. God loves you. You are special. God bless you in abundance.

You have always been there for us in our hours of need and now you have a huge battle on your hands. We can only offer you our prayers and support during this time. You have always shown great sympathy and understanding plus a willingness to give issues your best shot. We hope these strengths of your will be there for you to call on now.

To dearest Father John,

If only I knew what to say I would. In the meantime the prayers of my whole family are with you through this illness. You are extremely dear to us and you are in our thoughts all the time. You have always been there for all of us and now I am sure that Jesus will make you well soon. The whole family loves you and we all trust in Jesus.

Dearest Father John,

During the course of our lives we sometimes have the good fortune of crossing paths of people who have brought light into our lives. A light that shall forever shine in our hearts and fill them with love and kindness towards each other. This light is you, Father John.

We thank you for bringing our community closer together, for always greeting us with your smile and a cheeky "Hello", enveloping us in your love. We thank you for always having time for us and for coming to Our Lady Help of Christians Parish. We thank you because we are better people for having met you. We thank God for having sent you to us and you shall forever remain in our hearts. We love you always. God bless you.

Dear Father John,

You are a wonderful spiritual leader and are in our prayers. I pray that God answers our prayers as we prepare to celebrate the birth of Jesus. I thank you so very much with all our love and prayers.

Dear Father,

Thanks so much for your support of us during 2012. Your compassion and care is much appreciated. Our prayers and thoughts are with you as you prepare for the challenges that lay ahead in 2013.

Dear Father John,

If I only knew what to say, I would. In the meantime the prayers of the whole family are with you through this illness. You are extremely dear to us and you are in our thoughts all the time. You have always been there for us and now I am sure that Jesus will make you well soon. The whole family loves you lots and we thank you for all you did for our father.

Dear John,

We will be with you every step of the way. Your life has been in constant support and devotion to others and now it is your time to allow all those who hold you dear to return this goodwill to you. I only ask that you take the time to focus on yourself, and only yourself, physically and mentally. Your journey now requires your full focus so give it unconditionally.

Someone once said to me that if there was anyone who could return those who were lost back to the church it was Father John and I truly believe this.

Dear Father John,

I want to wish you the very best during your cancer treatment. My prayer is that the medicos can devise a way of returning you to good health again very quickly. Thank you for the impact you have had on our parish - the benefits will be far reaching in a way only a person such as you could initiate change on such a large scale. I hope you can leave the concerns of everybody else behind you and now concentrate on yourself and your recovery. May God bless you and hold you gently during your difficult days. Thank you for everything.

Joffa,

Here's a few things I picked up and worked out along the way. I hope they help.

DEHYDRATION is your mortal enemy. Drink plenty of water

DON'T PUSH YOURSELF. Listen to your body and give it the rest it needs. To fight your body is to lose.

DON'T WASTE ENERGY by worrying about the things you can't control, or with people and things that aren't important. Focus all your energy on the task at hand.

COUNT YOUR BLESSINGS EVERY DAY. Even the smallest gestures can be the source of gratitude and energy.

And remember, you're not dead, you're not dying. YOU'RE ALIVE.

Dear John,

We pray for you regarding treatment. I feel sorry for people who don't have God in their lives. I am sure God hears me coming and thinks, "When does this woman sleep?" I wake up each day with the rosary beads either down the bottom of the bed or wound around my hands. How do people survive without their faith? I'm sure God hears me coming and thinks, "Not again!" What great support one has through prayers. I'm sure he understands. Please God you stay as well as can be. With all our love and prayers.

Just to remember who you are makes a difference to so many people. We love and care about you. Thanks John for being you.

Dear Father John,

I am sorry to hear of your illness. I don't understand why this happens to an amazing man as yourself. The impact you have had on our lives is beyond words - your personality, your caring nature and your special way of making people feel important, draws people to you. The amount of lives you have touched is fantastic. We will pray for your recovery every day, as we know too well what the power of prayer can do. Thank you for your constant prayers and support. May God and all your family and friends help you on this journey. I still remember the first time I met you. It was at a friend's wedding about 13 years ago and I remember thinking what an amazing priest you are. Your love and faith shone through that day. We are very lucky to have you at our parish. You are a wonderful person and a brilliant priest. Our love and prayers always.

I am so pleased that you are with your sister and that you have some one to care for you. I hope that this Christmas season is a season of blessing for you from heaven above, a season of sharing with all those we love, a season of caring and warmth and good cheer, a season of hope for the coming new year. John, I have always known you to have a very strong mind and to make good decisions. The scans and the treatment will be decided for you and I hope it won't make you too sick, but now there are tablets to help you along.

God bless you, love and prayers.

Dear John,

We are thinking of you all the time and we know you will be able to rejoice in this lovely season despite your anxieties. Hopefully they will be diminishing as the doctor proceeds with your treatments.

Dear Father John,

I had prayed and prayed to the Holy Spirit to enlighten me as I heard about your cancer and that you had resigned from your parish at Koo Wee Rup. I was so pleased I had an address to write to. What words to say at this time of sorrow. Losing your independence and the shock of it all. John I have been praying to Mary MacKillop and Mary the Mother of our Saviour to plead with the Father for you at this time of great stress. I say this poem every morning for cancer patients. It goes like this:

What cancer cannot do

Cancer is so limited
It cannot cripple love
It cannot shatter hope
It cannot corrode faith
It cannot destroy peace
It cannot fill friendship
It cannot suppress memories
It cannot silence courage
It cannot invade the soul
It cannot steal eternal life
It cannot conquer the spirit

Dear Father John,

I was so sorry to hear of your serious illness and I write to assure you of my prayers at this time. You have been an inspiration to many and it is now our turn to support you and thank you for your ministry to many.

Our Dearest Father John,

Just a few words to let you know that you are constantly in our thoughts and daily prayers and we pray for a miracle and also for God to give you the strength and peace of mind to know that God is always with you. We will pray for a speedy recovery and full healing from our Lord and saviour. God bless you abundantly Father John.

Dear Father John,

I came to know about your ill health and I'm deeply sorry to hear of it. My family and I would like to give the comfort of knowing that we care. Have faith, have strength, have courage. You will beat this. You are in our thoughts and prayers.

Dearest Father John,

During the course of our lives we sometimes had the good fortune of crossing paths of people who have brought light into our lives. A light that shall forever shine in our hearts and fill them with love and kindness towards each other. This light is you, Father John.

Dear John,

The news just reached me of your sickness and I thought I would let you know that you are very much in our prayer and thoughts. Thank you so much for your support and friendship to all the Cluny Sisters.

Hello Father John,

Sending you my love and all God's blessings with it too. You have been such a fantastic priest, so broadminded and ever so reachable. You never question but you support the lowly. You are being missed so much by so many people already. Be strong and let the will of God sustain you. It is difficult this journey of yours, but he who endures to the end will be saved. God be with you and do pray for me to overcome as well.

It was so lovely to see you at your healing Mass and with so many people in your corner praying for you and offering support it must have been very uplifting. The cancer diagnosis is such a shock. I received that news 12 months ago and it is very hard to believe that it can happen to you. Then the whirlwind of doctors, hospital and treatment that come next is a roller coaster in itself. Stay well my friend and know we are all praying for your speedy recovery.

I want you to know that you remain the focus of prayers with the students, staff members and parents. Father John, you know God walks this journey with you. You remain a great inspiration to us all in so many ways.

Dearest John,

To be loved is important. You are so lucky!

John, in the midst of all your pain and suffering you still find time to pray for your flock. You are an inspiration and a true shepherd.

We thank you for bringing our community closer together, for always greeting us with your smile and a cheeky "Hello", enveloping us in your love. We thank you for always having time for us and for coming to Our Lady Help of Christians Parish. We thank you because we are better people for having met you. We thank God for having sent you to us and you shall forever remain in our hearts. We love you always. God bless you.

The students at school continue to ask after you and pray for you. You have left an awesome presence at all three schools and parishes and we MISS you!

Sending you all of our love and best wishes. We re-watched our wedding video recently (on our first wedding anniversary) and we cried. It was the perfect day! You are such an important part of our lives and our marriage, and you made our day really special.

Dear Father John,

Our national Novena to St Mary of the Cross ended this morning but I and many other parishioners who love you are going to continue the prayer for your recovery. Anything is possible to God. All we need to do is trust Him in total surrender. With so many friends praying for you over this country plus Fathers Francis and Joseph in Nigeria, we hope that our prayers will be heard according to the gracious will of God. Trust, hope, relax!

Father John,

We were saddened to hear of your ill health and can only say how much we love you. Father John, we will pray each day that you will recover. It will be a difficult time with medical procedures but you will bounce back, please God. Love.

Dearest Father John,

This is a difficult time for you and your family. It is also a difficult time for us, your friends, to know that your health is not 100%. Nevertheless you are always in our thoughts and prayers and we hope that everything will work out well. Stay strong and positive. Take care and may God bless you and your family.

Dear Father John,

You are the funniest and best story-telling priest ever. Get better soon.

Our Dearest Father John,

Just remember you are in our thoughts and prayers. We love you and are forever grateful for all you have done for us. We know that miracles can happen. God loves you. You are special. God bless you in abundance. Lots of love.

Dearest John,

Thank you for the gift you have been to our family - always there to serve and rejoice in our important milestones, births, marriages and grief. You will always be a part of our family, close to our hearts and prayers. We love you and always will.

Dear Father John,

Easter greetings. Essendon won! Get well. We need you.

Hi John,

Just to say "Hello". This tiny shell was found along the Lakes Entrance shores when I went walking there last week. Keep safe. Love

Dear Father John,

Remember Sarah? You gave her the opportunity to study at Don Bosco Primary School. Well, Sarah will be in Grade 5! God bless you always. Thank you for all you have done for us. We will pray for you.

Dearest John,

May Easter re-awaken the promises of the risen Lord and give you peace, hope and joy. I have delayed writing because it is too hard. Nothing I can say will make it any easier for you, but I don't want you to think that I have forgotten you or that we don't care. I hope the effects of the chemo are as intended and the side effects minimal. We know that your family will be surrounding you with love and support but we ask that you call on us if there is anything we can do.

Dear John,

I want to let you know that we continue to pray for you and that you are very much on our minds. A couple of weeks ago I was fortunate to go on retreat at Santa Casa in Queenscliff. It was all on Thomas Morton whom I had previously given very little thought, but he was an amazing man who wrote prolifically about God's love. I enjoy reading some of his works. And of course, to be right on the beach was an amazing experience of how God uses all things to reveal His love. I just wanted to let you know that we care for you and love you very much and will continue to pray for you.

We hope you are feeling better. You are in our prayers. We used to live in Narre Warren and you blessed us for our 50th wedding anniversary.

I worked at the Nursing Home and I remember that awful man we were nursing who wouldn't let the Asian girls near him. He used to shout at them, "Get out black bitch!" He was dying and yelling for a priest. I telephoned you and you came straight away in your shorts, to the amusement of the nurses who thought that priests always dressed like Bing Crosby in the movies. So that old B--- might just have got inside the Pearly

Gates because of you. You are remembered in my prayers.

Dear John,

I believe that there is a beached whale near Lakes Entrance. We have been to Geelong's old ground. The new stand and the lights are fantastic. I don't even need a cushion for my seat, and plenty of legroom. The Bombers are still going well and will make the finals even though there is a bit of controversy. No doubt you will do your best to see them play. Hopefully they won't beat the Cats! May the Lord's healing power be showered upon you with his strengthening touch. With our love and prayers.

We continue to think of you and pray for you. Thanks for keeping us updated on your blog; that is very generous of you. Peter Stringfellow spoke of you this morning and you received rousing applause. I have a small insight through my own illness about how you must feel – too deep to write about, but just know that we care deeply and trust our love and prayers to support you in the mysterious way that faith does. A great optimism and hope seems to be spreading through Pope Francis' election. Thank God as we can all do with this lift in our church. Our love care and support is with you, John.

Hang in there, John. I know that things can be hard at times but just do your best and hang in there. I am sorry you are going through a tough time right now. My heart goes out to you with affection, and also faith that everything will be okay. You are such a special person, so capable and caring and I know you will be able to handle the challenges that lie ahead. You can count on one thing. We love and care for you and keep you in our hearts, hoping and praying for brighter days to come. If anyone deserves a wealth of beautiful tomorrows then that special person is you John.

Friendship is not a big thing. It is lots of little things. Thank you Father John.

Dear Father John,

This card comes with lots of love and prayers for you at this time of your life. I do not know or understand why God allows such a prolonged time of pain but we do believe he answers prayers for fortitude to bear the pain. We think of you all the time and must not only pray for a miracle but also for a safe journey home if that is what God wants.

Dear John,

I hope you have switched off from your parish work. Quiet time is good for the healing process. No doubt you have discovered the ups and downs of being a cancer patient. Savour the moment, relax and do things you enjoy. One of the things I learnt was to listen to my body and when it said, "Not today", then it was "No". A cancer patient becomes more aware of the preciousness of life and learns that little things don't matter. God's gift of life is wonderful. "Behold a treasure not made of gold." Love life to the fullest John and know you are more precious than gold as we prepare for Easter.

Dear Father Allen,

We are thinking of you and keeping you in our prayers. May you be reminded how you are loved and cared for by us all. Sending lots of courage and hope.

Dear Father John,

You and all your loved ones have been in my heart and prayers. For many years your parents prayed for a sister of mine and her husband when they were struggling and great things happened. So John, we live in hope that you will be well in God's good time.

Thank you Father John for all you have done for myself and my family. We are all praying for you and ask God to restore you to perfect health. Father John, you answered the call of the spirit and served your people well.

Just to let you know you are in our thoughts and prayers for a speedy recovery. We met 21 years ago in Morwell when you baptised our son. Such a lot of time has passed and you were there for his First Confession, Communion and Confirmation and also for our daughter. You gave the most wonderful sermons and are a most wonderful man, despite your choice of football team! Get well as we look forward to sharing our next important family event with you.

Dear Father John,

You have been an important role model to me since I was a baby. I always enjoyed going to church because I knew you would be there and would treat everybody kindly and make everyone laugh. You are such a gentle and caring man, and I truly hope you get better soon.

Dear John,

Easter is fast approaching as we welcome Pope Francis and footy is about to begin. I wonder if we at Essendon can do a 'Black Caviar'?

Hello Father John,

We do hope you are having more good days than bad as we read your bit in the bulletin. We always think of you. I saw a white heron, near where I walk. It was flying across the swamp outside the kitchen, a magnificent sight – so clean, elegant and swift. I do hope all is well with you and you are enjoying family and friends. Did you hear about the Irish fish? It drowned!

We will miss you terribly John. But let's not miss you yet. We still have time to love you and be with you.

Dear John,

We are all sorry to hear that you are unwell. We hope that you are being looked after at the hospital. John, thank you so much for the wonderful and special brother you have been for my wife. And thank you for being a really important part of our children's lives – they have always loved your presence, your great sense of humour and your great commitment to your faith and to the Bombers! Thank you for marrying us and for being a really important part of my life also. With very special wishes and lots of love.

May you be given the courage and strength to carry your cross. I was a part of the small group of visitors when you began the Baptism program all those years ago in the Morwell Parish. I am sure you have a lot of support and prayers throughout the Sale Diocese and beyond.

Dear John,

Thank you for the blessing you have been to myself, my parents and my brother and sister throughout the years. And thank you for your great contribution to my faith through weekly Mass, Confession and Confirmation. You are in my prayers. God bless you.

I hope you are getting better and that Easter is a good time for you. Thank you for being part of our lives.

Dear John,

Thank God for the lovely warm sun after the cold frosty night. When this arrives I hope you have been able to conquer the nausea. I don't think any person escapes that sick feeling that goes with chemo. One learns to cope with it. Distract yourself and of course take the medication that is given to you. Bombers are still hanging in there and long may they continue. I wonder if Fletch should step aside before we lose another game. Thinking of you and praying that you will improve particularly health wise. May God in his goodness keep you close to Him.

To let you know that we are storming heaven for you. Living is fun. Look at what Essendon has done to the footy! Don't worry, the others are shaking in their boots. Take each day as it comes knowing the Lord is with you always.

Big news about Pope Benedict and now the election of Pope Francis. His Holiness has been accepted on all sides of the world and seems to be a very humble man, no wonder he chose Francis as a name. We miss you not being with us very much and look forward to your return but don't rush, take plenty of time to recover and then come back.

We heard that you weren't well and hope and pray that God gives you strength, courage and lots of reminders that He is always with you, supporting and loving you.

I ask that He be near you at the start of each day, but I pray most of all for His loving care. Wishing you the blessing to have the courage and peace of mind to face life and all its trials that come your way.

We will always be grateful to you for helping us through a very difficult time for us in 2010.

We heard that you are unwell and are thinking of you. John you have been such a strong influence in our lives. We are both from families that are true believers and this was instilled in us when we were young. However, when we were in our twenties and with a young family attending Don Bosco, we felt a stronger connection with God because of your leadership at this time. You have a gift with children and couples like us. We thank you for this as we have been able to bring our children up in the same way our parents did, to share their lives with God. We are so proud of this.

Sometimes for prayer to be effective, it has to be prayed many times. I am praying hard. Happy Easter.

We wanted to share with you some photos of our son. He is doing so well and as God has blessed us with this joy, we wanted to share it with you, hoping it would breathe some happiness and respite into your life at this difficult time. Our baby is six months old now and smiles and giggles to our delight. He loves rocking to "Row, row, row your boat," and babbles a lot. He is learning to eat mashed up food and is close to rolling over independently. We are in awe of his potential for learning and growth when we watch him. We often reflect on the protective love we have for him and the enormous trust he has in us. Only a snowdrop when compared to God's great love and the trust we have in Him. We are humbled. You are always in our prayers and in our hearts.

Dear Father John,

I was saddened to hear how ill you are and hope you are not in too much pain. I will always think of you and your special caring ways and how when my husband was dying you would pop in for a cuppa and a piece of my fruitcake. The night he died we sat on the bed afterwards and said some prayers and had a little sherry and then you helped the undertaker, as it was difficult to get through the hallway door. You stayed with me afterwards. No wonder everybody admired you. You were so special, friendly and just Father John, a lovely man who would always be there with a smile and who did a great job around Narre Warren. I will always think of you as a good friend who has done a lot for my family.

To our very dear Father John,

You have been part of our church community and we miss you Father. Please God look after our dear Father John and make him better soon. This message is sent with fond love.

An Easter prayer, John, that in the love of Christ you will be blessed with the power of His healing. A heart full of wishes with abundance of love and thank you's.

I thank you for your prayers during my illness and your cheery attitude that has helped me get through. I love this Psalm, 107 – 19, 20: "I cried unto you my Lord in my trouble and you saved me out of my distress. You sent your word and healed me and delivered me from my destruction." We know that your courage and faith will get you through this and we look forward to even better meetings at parties and social occasions as we are confident with all your prayers and ours and the rest of the community and congregation you will be well again soon.

Trust you are enjoying the beauty and warmth of Lakes. You are doing a great job in handling it all. Life is precious and so are you. Keep on keeping on.

We were so shocked when we first heard your news. You have a battle on your hands and I can't imagine what must be going on for you. You, John, have always been one of our 'favourites'. You epitomize the best of Priesthood and we have often commented on your great positivity and humour, two qualities (and many others) you will no doubt bring to your treatment. Wishing a fine man all the blessings in the coming months.

We all send our love and best wishes as your journey unfolds. John, you hold a very special place in our family's hearts. Oh, and if you ever have any difficulty with any of your meds, just give Essendon a call!

I hope you continue to improve and that the chemo is doing its job. It is a slow process that needs to take its time and I always say accept it as a friend. Wasn't it a good game on Friday night? The local pub has attracted many more patrons since the new owners took over. That, for sure, is good for the town. May the red and black keep on flying even if it's the last breath of the game. You had better take it a little easy on your walking on these cold frosty mornings. Look out for yourself.

We just wanted to say thank you for baptising our baby boy and welcoming him into our extended family. We are so grateful that you have been such an important part of all the great celebrations in our lives, imbuing them with such love, humour and meaning. We love you.

Lots of love and prayers for you at this time. I do not understand why God allows such a prolonged period of pain but I do believe he answers prayers and we think of you all the time. I will be bombarding the heavens but I must accept that I must not only pray for a miracle but also for a safe journey home if that is what God wants.

Dear Father John,

I was devastated to hear the news of your pancreatic cancer and I hope and pray that you will have a full recovery. I remember how kind you were to my family when my father took his own life. Please fight it with all you have and I will pray the Novena for you.

Dear Father John,

Our love and prayers are with you as you continue your journey for a better life. May the peace of God be with you and keep you going. Your football team won today to give you a lift. Like you, they are having a few problems but it should work out in the end. Keep your chin up and hope things will be more bearable for you. God's blessing to help you. All our prayers are with you.

Father John,

You were not only a mentor for me but also a friend. Every time I saw you, even if it had been a while between seeing you, it felt like it had been yesterday. You were important in my family and even my parents, who are not Catholic - Mum calls herself agnostic - respected you for the man you are and for the care and concern which you showed towards me and, particularly in the last year, my son.

Everything has a reason. When you came to our shop to have a haircut, I believe that God sent you. I believe that my family and me met you because Jesus wanted us to, such a nice and gentleman person. We miss you and you are always in my morning prayer and I am waiting for you to come for your next haircut.

This is a photo that was taken on one of the most memorable days of my life - my wedding. The day would not have been complete without you, John. You have been there for everything, for myself and my family.

I could write a novel on what you mean to me. My eight-year-old son said, "Father John will always be a wonderful man in our hearts."

Father John,

You were my rock in good times and in bad. You reached out to all, not only those in your parish but to everyone. Everyone was welcome.

Thank you for the companionship and support that you gave me throughout my time of working with you at the seminary. It was wonderful! They were good times, the best of times really, and made so by you with such good humour, fun, lots of laughs and wise guidance too. We worked well together! Now in these difficult days what can I say? I am so sad really, but I know too that you have a strong and deep faith to face up to this part of your journey. Certainly I am close to you in prayer each day, trying to trust that the letting go will not be too difficult, for you or for us. You are loved so much by so many John - a great priest and a person of great humanity.

RAINBOW OVER NARRE WARREN

Only God knows the way for you
Only God knows the time
Into His hands I know you will lovingly place yours
God's way is love

John finds his way home

The cancer had been suspected, diagnosed, confirmed. The MRI had been completed, the biopsy had been done.

"Not good news," announced the treating doctor. "You have pancreatic cancer, one that we just haven't been able to tame as yet. With treatment you can count on six to nine months; without, perhaps three months."

So treatment was planned, but couldn't be started just then as Christmas was upon us, the festive season and holidays were about to begin.

"We will start in the new year," was the instruction. "Go home and enjoy Christmas, take it easy and get your affairs in order."

We, his family, heard it, but didn't comprehend. It was happening but it didn't seem to be true. John went home, compiled a list of his few possessions, made a Last Will & Testament ensuring that each of his nine siblings received some small gift from him and settled into his final journey.

"I don't want to go yet! I love life. It is fun," he pleaded with his maker. "Perhaps if I pray to Mary

MacKillop a miracle might happen. I may be cured."

Other ideas were canvassed.

"Is it beneficial to eat asparagus?" he asked his attending physician, because a well-wisher had told him that it was a proven cure. "Only if you like asparagus," came the reply from the grey, humourless oncologist, worn down from daily interaction with the dying. After 20 years on the job and with three children at private schools he could only survive by thinking of the next weekend bike ride or the kayaking holiday in South America. Men with pancreatic cancer did not survive. He knew that and didn't believe in miracles.

But John's faith was strong and he believed that he had served the Lord with all his might and that there was still more to do in his earthly ministry. He prayed fervently, his friends and family interceded on his behalf, his parishioners organized Novenas to the saints, strangers from other parts of the country pleaded with God for a cure. They stormed heaven with their prayers. "Please God, keep John with us," was their mantra. "We want a miracle."

His spiritual advisor suggested: "We must be positive, for hope is all we have. Miracles happen, but not always in the way we earthly creatures imagine. Trust in God."

The short journey had begun. Christmas came. His family gathered around and affirmed him, never actually believing that this was the last festive season the 10 of them would spend together.

"John loves his God and God loves John. He must get a miracle," they rationalized, believing that John was special and would be spared death.

He resigned his parish and returned to his boyhood home, a beautiful place with water and lakes all around, to recuperate between the treatments.

"Concentrate on getting well. Be positive. Enjoy your family and friends. God works in mysterious ways," counselled his advisor.

Chemo treatments began. John became medicalized. Every week to the hospital, every week a struggle to find a vein to attached a drip that spewed forth poison. Healing poison. Always at the chemist's, getting tablets for this side effect, medicine for that one; feeling weak, burning inside, a nauseous sensation, tiredness that creeps all over. Keep on going, smile, don't let people worry, pretend to be well, can't be a burden, stay positive.

Three months pass. The first scan: a joyous occasion. "The primary cancer has reduced; things are going well, celebrate for tomorrow things could change," the world-weary doctor smiled weakly, knowing the truth.

A wonderful night with family ensued when all was well with the world and the cancer seemed to be beaten. Mary MacKillop was doing her work.

Perhaps she was enjoying her saintly duties and John was her new work-in-progress. He was so happy his feet barely touched the ground. Thank you God! Life is so precious!

Another month. Treatment continues. Gradually feeling weaker, but smile on. Don't make anybody worry. Pretend to be well. The football has started for the year and he can sit in 'Big Chair' and watch his beloved team. But Essendon is in disarray. They did whatever it took to win and it was not good. A cancer had struck the club and they were in big strife. He felt sad. Time to let go. He had enjoyed them while he lived but time was running out and he didn't need to spend precious chunks of it worrying about earthly things. He stopped praying for a cure and began to pray for a safe journey home.

"Please God let me be strong enough to endure what is ahead, to suffer as you suffered and to come home to you," he asked.

"I will ensure that you do not feel pain," promised the oncologist while mentally planning his next weekend road race.

His family resisted. "We don't want John to die. We need him here with us. He is our brother. It is not his turn. Of his nine siblings there are four who are older than he is." Some were in denial, others numb with disbelief, while others put aside their fears and determined he should be allowed to die in the way he wanted.

His friends rallied and spent time with him. He gathered his strength and baptised his new grand nephew and namesake, Jonty. The whole family was invited but some didn't realize the significance so didn't come. The ones who did witnessed John in his last priestly role. So precious, so John, this was what he did on earth. He was exhausted from the effort and returned to his home.

That weekend, his own body fluids collapsed his lung and made him aware that the final leg of the journey had begun. Alone and drowning within himself, he took his mind away from his suffering by researching the readings for his funeral, organizing the music and allocating as many of his family members as possible a duty on the day of his burial. He was admitted to the local hospital.

"Drain him off and send him home," advised the careworn oncologist when phoned for instructions.

"I won't do that. He needs special care, he is a very sick man," argued the caring local doctor.

"Put him in an ambulance and send him down to me then."

He was admitted to the city hospital and never came out. A fortnight of procedures and suffering, endured with patience and good humour. Visitors, cards, good wishes flooded the shared room for it was school holidays and the good doctor was not there to advocate that this dying man have the privacy of his own room. He was off riding his bike.

Then a clot that had been causing the blockages moved and went to his lung.

"Come quickly, John is dying." His family was summoned. Those who could, came and held his hand, incredulous that it had come to this.

"John would you like to say the rosary?"

"John would you like us to sing a hymn?"

"No, just keep talking to each other. Talk about ordinary things. And I will listen," he panted as he struggled for breath.

"Keep calm and breathe deeply," said one of his sisters. "Dying, like birthing, is a part of living. Mum did it ten times. You can do it. Stay calm and let your body do the work."

John laboured and when he was about to breathe his last he pulled off the oxygen mask and panted in a strained voice, "I want you to know that I love you all."

And then he went to God.

He was home.

- E. J.

Final phone messages

These messages were left on John's mobile phone, the night he died, 12th July 2013.

11:55 AM on July 12, 2013

When it is said that everyone has a purpose in this life there is no doubt that Father John Allen achieved this and more. The love and guidance and inspiration he has given to so many has been a true gift. May he have left this world with the most accepting and peaceful heart and enveloped with love on his journey to his eternal home. May prayers and faith help to carry his beautiful loving family in this time of loss. May they find the acceptance and comfort in memories they need. Endless love and gratitude to a wonderful man. REST IN PEACE.

12:22 AM on July 13, 2013

Father John, you were a true example of how fellow man should be. Always caring, never saying "No" to those in need and always greeting everyone with your warm smile. You made our parish what it is today. Everyone loved coming to Mass to be welcomed by you. You were never bothered by the cries of children, by people walking in late, you were just glad that they were part of the church. My family and I, like so many others, will miss you dearly but we will never forget you. Our thoughts are with your family. REST IN PEACE, Father John.

1:40 AM on July 13, 2013

After literally decades of wandering in the wilderness, it was Father John Allen who reached out and gathered me into his flock. This kind and gentle shepherd was then ever ready to guide me whenever I looked like straying off the correct path once more. And it was our very great honour when this true and devoted servant of the Lord married us before God just a few short years ago. Molly and I will miss you, Father John. May you now gaze upon the face of God, and rest gently in His bosom.

4:30 AM on July 13, 2013

Rest in peace Father John. The Catholic Church has truly lost a great shepherd. Words can't express how much you will be missed and how dear you were to all of us. We will forever remember you and keep you in our prayers.

6:48 AM on July 13, 2013

RIP Father John Allen, you were a wonderful man with great faith that had a church overflowing to hear you, and friends coming out of all corners of the world. May you rest in peace with your maker. You will be sadly missed by one and all. XXX.

7:44 AM on July 13, 2013

RIP Father John. God is with you but we have lost you. A wonderful, wonderful priest in this 21st Century. Heartbroken, with condolences to the family of Father John. RIP that smiling face.

1:09 AM on July 13, 2013

Eternal rest grant unto Father John, oh Lord, may his soul rest in peace.

You were a great priest, a gentleman and a fantastic human being. We were privileged to have known you and truly blessed to have enjoyed your friendship.

May you enjoy a well-deserved entry to eternal life in paradise. God bless.

11:31 PM on July 12, 2013

John, you may no longer be here physically but you will always be here with us in our memories and our love. We miss you dreadfully. You are now at peace and we will never forget you. See you in Lakes at every turn.

Thank you God for Father John

Now Father John is gone
Our grief is deep but his work goes on
This man so connected and loved
Is safely home with God above
John penned a message when his time had come
To thank Narre Warren for all they had done
"To my family, friends and parishioners
Who have prayed for me over all these years
When you come this way, you will not be alone
I will not forget you in my heavenly home."
Thank you God for Father John
May his dear spirit live on and on

- E. J.

John penned his last words

The weekend before he was admitted to hospital, Father John was alone and so sick he thought he was going to die there and then. He penned this message to be read at his funeral.

This is like a message coming from the other side, but I think it's important to say.

My illness came suddenly, like a thief in the night.

But what at the start seemed like a disaster has brought many blessings.

My family, who have always loved and supported me in my life and in my work as a priest, have been so marvellous in their love and care for me.

It has lifted me up and carried me on eagle's wings during this time of adjustment and acceptance.

I will not mention anyone by name, because I include every family member. Sisters, brothers, brothers-in-law and sister-in-law; my nieces and nephews, grand nieces and nephews. To everyone, thank you, you will not be forgotten in my heavenly home.

To the bishop and priests of the diocese, I thank you for your support and acceptance of me during my years as a priest - years that I have loved - and would not do anything different.

I was happy to be a priest; it is a most happy and fulfilling life. To my friends and parishioners, who have prayed for me over all these years, I will not forget you.

RAINBOW OVER NARRE WARREN

Father John Allen
*Ordained to the Catholic Priesthood
Sale, Victoria,
August 19th 1978.
Worked as assistant priest or parish priest in
the following parishes:
Maffra, Sale, Lakes Entrance,
Traralgon, Yarram, Morwell, Narre Warren,
Koo Wee Rup/Iona/Maryknoll.
He also worked at Corpus Christi Seminary in
Clayton and on various Diocesan committees
and boards.
He served his people well.*

*Father John was honoured to say his First Mass in the community hall in Lakes Entrance, amongst the people with whom he grew to manhood.
The township was proud of the hometown boy and they turned out in force to celebrate this great moment with him. Their generosity overwhelmed him. It was a wonderful occasion.
All of his life John loved Lakes Entrance and its people. That is where he retreated between treatments when he was diagnosed with his insidious cancer. Its beauty soothed his soul.*

157

Father John, centre at back, with staff from the hub of all activity at Narre Warren, the Parish Centre.

Father John doing what he loved to do most – celebrating the Eucharist.

Above: Father John particularly enjoyed child-centred celebrations such as First Communion.
Below: Celebrating the wonderful diversity of Narre Warren Parish.

*Above: Showing how it's done. Father John, the 'Karaoke King,' enjoying a parish function.
Below: John's parents knew and enjoyed meeting many of John's parishioners. They often attended Mass and celebrations in his parishes. Here is John with his father Jack.*

Above: Father John, looking a little embarrassed as he is caught on camera taking care of the flowers for a bride while photos are taken.
Below: John and Sister Gail Ryan enjoy a chat on the occasion of his Silver Jubilee in the Priesthood.

Above: Before his ordination, John with his sister Mary and niece Caitlin (Johnstone) Hobbs at Morwell 1975.
Below: John with his brothers and father, circa 1980. Arthur (left), Jack, John, Robert.

Father John presided over the religious rights and ceremonies of his huge extended family as well as his parishioners, previous parishioners and many friends. He never said 'No' to anybody. He married his siblings Maureen, Arthur, Mary and Eileen, and baptised and married most of the 32 nieces and nephews, as well as numerous grand nieces and nephews, cousins and second cousins. He also buried the dead. He did all this with compassion, humour and goodwill, never complaining although often stretched by parish duties and other commitments.
He gave his time generously to all.

Above: With grand niece Jaimee Morrison after her Baptism in Bairnsdale in 1994.
Below: Officiating at sister Mary's wedding in Lakes Entrance in 1986.

The family gathered in Koo Wee Rup in November 2012 for John's 60th birthday. It was to be his last. He was diagnosed with cancer a week later.

In May 2013 John performed his final priestly duty. He baptised his namesake, grand nephew Jonty (Little John) Wilson. The cancer had swollen his belly and he was very ill, but there is a peaceful joy in his face. He loved doing it. "This is the last time I will wear these robes," he said. He was right.

Tribute to a great pilgrim

Narre Warren parish pastoral assistant Dina Mananquil–Delfino penned a moving tribute to Father John in her 'Philippine Times' column on July 22nd 2013.

There are many people who come into our lives. Some fade into the background of our memories, while others leave a lasting impression. On the 12th of July 2013, I got a text message that Father John Allen, a dear friend and our parish priest at Narre Warren for almost 16 years passed away at about 7:30 pm after battling with pancreatic cancer for six months. The overnight trip I had with Boy to celebrate our 29th year anniversary took a quick turn from a joyful mood into a sad evening filled with text messages, as the whole community tried to grapple in disbelief.

At 60, Father John was relatively young and although he had been a priest for 35 years, we felt that there was still much he could accomplish.

To us, he was always larger than life. He was LOVE exemplified. To his large family (belonging to 10 siblings) and 49 grand nieces and nephews, he was the devoted son, brother, cousin, uncle whose inspiring fidelity included being there for every family event. To his colleagues, Father John was an unassuming yet learned friend and mentor, gifted with words of encouragement. To the Essendon Bombers, he was the passionate fan, whose homilies included a footy update, embracing a keen interest in human activities. To his flock, he was the good shepherd, anointed by Jesus to continue His work of love, always giving, authentic and blessed with an astounding memory.

He touched many families whether that encounter was a simple blessing of their home, car, pet or a sick family member, celebrating the sacraments, or just plain visiting and dining with them. As families shared their crises he only had one word - LOVE as Jesus loves.

As a friend, he showed how much he enjoyed company. We proclaimed him Karaoke King when he scored 100 for 'Paper Roses', beating Boy's 99 for 'Delilah'! It was a title he esteemed with much fun. Like St Paul, he was everything to everyone. "Good on ya!" was his cheer.

The outpouring of losing him had come to us in many ways. The first one occurred when he was transferred - many cried. Then when he died, the pain was profoundly deeper. About 2000 people showed their affection and respect at his Vigil and Requiem Masses at Narre Warren and Lakes Entrance, where he is now buried with his mum, dad, and brother-in-law.

Two weeks before he passed away, I had a chance to visit him in hospital. Despite feeling unwell, he received us graciously, allowing us the humbling privilege to pray with him, hug him and express our love. He asked only for prayers for a peaceful pilgrimage home and booked my brother-in-law Rey and sister Tes for their music. We persevered, praying for a physical miracle and the whole parish continued storming heaven. But the Lord has other plans, often beyond human understanding.

Now in total surrender, we can only thank God for giving Father John to us for those many years, a man who showed how it is to live truthfully and how it is to die courageously. As we were gathered at Narre Warren, I saw a vision of him and my mum (he concelebrated Mum's Requiem Mass last year). I notice that more and more pilgrims from our parish are going home. It is comforting to have Father John with them. I realise it would be selfish of me to hold on to him.

That same night of our special tribute, I received a call from a friend that her niece, 16, took her life. My heart broke again. I am sure Father John, the good shepherd he is, will comfort this young girl as he asks the loving Father for mercy and salvation. Father John's website when he started to be ill was called 'Pilgrim's Progress'. We know even if his earthly pilgrimage is over, his heavenly work is just beginning.

Genuine and true, John saw everyone's importance

While his enjoyment of and attention to people and the everyday goings on in the parish was clearly apparent and widely appreciated, Father John always paid attention to the spiritual and prayer side of life.

Aiding him in this over more than two decades was his spiritual advisor, Brigidine Sister, Gail Ryan. Here she writes of the man she knew.

Much has been said about this extraordinary man but to me John was just my dear friend. I didn't ever think about his qualities, I just knew them. He was genuine and true. When in his company you were the most important person in the world. He treated everyone that way, always with dignity and respect. Yes, John was a man of many talents but maybe his greatest gift was his ability to bring the best out in people - a rare gift but a very important one. He enjoyed other peoples' successes and celebrated with them in their achievements, no matter how big or small!

John loved life and he loved people. He enjoyed attending the arts, particularly live shows with friends. He also loved travelling - both in Australia and overseas - and walking early each morning for an hour or so, meeting people along the way. Visiting his beloved parishioners was always high on his to-do list and he was always keenly interested in, and positive, when talking about the primary and secondary schools in his various parishes.

It was obvious to me that John came from a very loving and unique family, always talking about family members and celebrating with them as each occasion arose. He was deeply interested in and proud of each member of the extended Allen family.

John was a most forgiving man other than when Collingwood beat Essendon in the football! He rarely held a grudge and always tried to look on the positive side of life, even when he was so ill. A day rarely goes by that he is not thought of in some way. He was a man true to his word and to his calling as a very pastoral, humane, inspirational, selfless and faith-filled priest. I feel proud and privileged to be counted as one of his special friends. My beautiful memories will live in my heart forever.

In the words of St. Cyprian:

Lord you gave him to us to be our joy and now you have taken him away from us.
We give him back to you without a murmur but our hearts are wrung with sorrow.

Rest in peace my friend.

Fond, friendly - and funny - memories of John

Across the years, John met, befriended, worked with or helped many thousands of people, both personally and professionally. All will testify to his giving personality, his ability to make things happen, and just the occasional foible ...

Here are some recollections from people whose lives John touched.

My friend John

I have been blessed greatly in knowing this priest. He was my confessor, mentor and friend and it was this man that executed his priestly duties outside of the church that endeared him to so many people. On many occasions there were times he amazed me with his knowledge and wisdom that helped and supported me in my faith. I can only relate back to this friendship, and to be invited to visit his hospital bed some three hours before his death was such an honour. Of course, we did not know that the end was so near, but he still had time for people and to concern himself with their problems.

We should not fill ourselves with remorse in his going, but instead should celebrate with him. For there is no doubt in my mind that this man is enjoying his rewards with his maker, for he is a saint! I have no problems with the fact that he is looking after his flock of Narre Warren.

Dear John, how proud I have been to know you, to have had you as a friend and now to know that you are with God, and that you are still looking over us.

My only concern is with your football side. You seem to have overlooked the tragic situation that they are in. If you could please employ Jesus with a few prayers on their behalf, it would be greatly appreciated!

There were so many things to laugh about with John. I wish my memory was as good as his was because there were so many funny things that happened over the years. Here are just a few of them:

A people person

No matter where we went it always amazed me the number of people that would come up to John to speak to him. One day we were at an Essendon practice match at Morwell, when he said, "Let's go for a walk around the ground." That walk would have taken us over an hour, as we were stopped every few metres by people he knew who wanted to talk. I understand that he had been Parish Priest there for some time, but these interruptions happened everywhere he went, often at the 'G', but also at the stations or on the train going to the football. He drew people to him.

Trevor, take this woman!

On another occasion we were playing at Etihad Stadium and Sister Doreen had come along. We got to the Southern Cross station and Doreen was struggling as she had some hip soreness. She called John to give her a hand. So there it was, John and Doreen walking down the platform with Doreen hanging on to John's arm as if they were husband and wife. John became very embarrassed with the situation and finally said in a shocked voice, "Doreen, someone might see us. Here, hang on to Trevor!" And with that he walked off ahead.

True or false

The 6 pm Mass was over and there were just a few of us left in the church building. Joe the sacristan was doing his final rounds turning off lights and locking things up. He came out of the ladies toilet block carrying a paper bag which he handed to John for inspection, saying, "I found these in there, do you know what they are?"

John looked and pondered, turned them this way and that, but had not the slightest idea. Along comes Sister Doreen who was shown the articles. She couldn't contain her merriment and burst into hysterical laughter. John was holding a pair of ladies falsies. He dropped them and went beetroot red.

Amid a lot of laughter and ribbing many ideas were canvassed for finding the owner. They could hang them on the fence like you do with baby's booties; they could put them in a tree for a bird to nest in; or use them to right a wonky table. In the end I suggested we put a 'lost and found' in the following week's newsletter to see who would come forward to claim them. If that failed we could put them on eBay and the profits could go to John!

Saucy conundrum

We were playing Collingwood at the 'G' and John had gone walkabout. Upon his return he put his foot dead square on a full sauce satchel that was lying on the ground. The sauce squirted up like a cut artery, spraying all over the back of the woman in front, who by the way, wasn't barracking for the Bombers. She was a vocal Pies supporter! John didn't know what to do. Should he tell her and offer to have the jacket dry cleaned? Should he quietly lean over and wipe it off with his handkerchief? I advised against that and suggested we ignore it and pretend that it hadn't happened at all.

Open Sesame!

John always took his radio to the football to listen to the commentary. On this day he reached into his pocket and pulled out his remote door opener and attempted to put it to his ear.

Predictions

John was a very passionate Essendon supporter but was prone to doubt and despair early in the game. On many occasions he would be depressed about the play and make dire predictions. "We are going to lose this by 60 points," he would gloomily predict. Or, "There is no way that our blokes will pull this one off!" Later in the day, when the team was in a winning position, his demeanour would improve considerably and he would be quite jovial. We would tease him by reminding him about what he had said early in the day. He always denied it vehemently saying, "I never said that! Trevor was the one that wanted to go home at half time! I kept him here!"

Mixed messages

We were travelling in India with a relieving driver whose English was not the best. I was sitting in the front alongside him. Denis and John were in the back. I introduced myself and asked the driver his name. He replied, "Aashil." It was difficult to hear in the back seat and later, missing a snippet of information, John in all his innocence, requested, "What was that again, Arsehole?" He thought that was the driver's name and was not amused in the slightest when Denis and I collapsed in laughter.

- *Trevor Scott.*

Our colleague John

We always had plenty to laugh about when Father John was in the office. They weren't always hilarious moments, but they were the everyday little things that made us chuckle and our working day pleasant. Here are three that I can recall.

The party shop

The parish was having a New Year's Eve dinner dance as a fundraiser. Father John, wanting to be helpful, volunteered to buy the balloons and decorations from the Party Shop in Hallam. So, off he went and back he came very quickly. The ladies in the office were very impressed with his ability to get there, purchase the necessary items and return in such a short time. But the man who had so confidently gone out, had returned a bit sheepish and red-faced. He had indeed driven to the brightly coloured building in Hallam and parked his car opposite. But lo and behold it was the Hallam Adult Party Shop! Needless to say I had to get the balloons myself.

The case of the missing keys

The Narre Warren Parish Office centre is a busy place during the day and evening with many meetings and gatherings. The parish had just installed a very high-tech security system and the staff was in the early stages of learning the ins and outs of it. One particular evening Father Matthew, the assistant priest, opened the office with his set of keys, went about doing a few things and then proceeded to a meeting in another room. After the meeting Father Matthew could not find his keys. As it was late, Father John locked up with his keys and they both went off to the presbytery, leaving the search for the missing keys until the morning. But a perplexed Father Matthew could not let this go and decided to put the high-tech security system to work. He was able to trace back to the exact times when he opened the office, finished his work, turned off the light and moved out of the office. All this was available visually on the system. Watching the tape further, determined to find out what has happened, he then spots Father John entering the scene, turning the light on, and going about entering stuff into the parish diary. Finishing his work, Father John then takes a set of keys off the door, puts them in his pocket, turns off the light and exits, locking the door. By now we have an audience of staff members fervently looking at the tape for every clue! When it is put to him, Father John denies that they are Matthew's keys and is convinced that they are his own. We decide to have a recall of keys. Guess what? Father John has two sets of keys in his pocket. Culprit found!

Wedding feast

I happened to be at a wedding reception where I was seated at a table with my mother, Father John and others. Father John knew my mum Iris well. During the speeches, which were lengthy, Father

John could not resist the nibbles on the table and helped himself to some of them. Mum seeing this, promptly smacked his hand and told him put back the nibbles and wait until the speeches were over. He did as he was told.

- Suzie Schumacher.

Faith, hope and love

"Faith, Hope and Love" is the motto of Trinity Catholic Primary School that was founded in the Jubilee Year of 2000. Father John's vision enabled this third primary school to be built in his parish and to become a witness of faith to the growing community of Narre Warren South.

I was the foundation principal of the school and these reflections are in the context of knowing John in this role. John's own life was a witness to the motto. He showed 'Faith' in trusting the inaugural staff of 13 dedicated people to build the school - not just bricks and mortar but as a place of faith and learning. We were all clear what John wanted of us. He expected commitment and dedication as well as expertise but once staff had been appointed, he did not interfere; rather, he listened and supported. I would like a dollar for every time I heard him say, "Sure, Mary." This translated as, "I believe you and endorse what you propose."

He inspired 'Hope'. There were many times when the task ahead was daunting. We had only a dusty, treeless paddock with a half-finished administration building and six old demountable classrooms to cater for the 129 new students who arrived on the first rainy day in February 2000. John was there, greeting parents and children in his calm, friendly way and encouraging us all as we began the journey to build a school.

And he had 'Love' in abundance. Children, staff and parents alike felt better in his presence. Class and school Masses were sources of inspiration where all felt accepted and valued.

In Shakespeare's 'Hamlet' Polonius advises, "Give each man thine ear but few thy voice." On several occasions I observed John rushing off to his next appointment but halting to listen to a parent or staff member who had stopped him with, "I know you're busy Father but could I just … " He always stopped to listen, then gave his reassuring "Sure" before going on his way. If it was an issue that needed more than a listening ear, he followed it up later. Either way, the applicant always went away feeling that he or she had been listened to.

My only point of difference with John was irreconcilable. He'd support me in staff appointments, applying for millions of dollars of grants, collaborating with architects for spending those dollars and all the various concerns that come with a rapidly growing school. But in the football season, I learnt that his passion for the Bombers was not to be challenged. I could never win an argument about football because his knowledge was far superior to mine, so we agreed to differ and I continued to follow the Saints and expected no mercy from John when they lost.

I enjoyed conversations about books, music, films and travel with him as well as about education. He epitomised for me, as for others, an example of a pastor, living out his faith, and helping others to know Jesus as he did.

John truly lived out St Paul's exhortation to the Corinthians. He also was an example of Adam Lindsay Gordon's verse:

> *Life is mostly froth and bubble*
> *Two things stand like stone*
> *Kindness in another's trouble*
> *Courage in your own*

John is honoured at Trinity via everyone's loving, grateful memories of him and in the building that is named in his honour.

- Mary Howlett.

Always part of our lives

We moved to Narre Warren from Springvale in 1993 and met Father John in 1996 after Father Denis left and when he became our Parish Priest.

Rey and I have been serving the Parish since 1993 by providing music at the 11 am Mass and in any parish activities that we can offer our services. In all these years, Father John was part of our lives. He saw how all our children and grandchildren grew into young adults and young kids. He knew all of them by name. He was part of every important family celebration, joyful and sad occasions. He prayed with us when my parents-in-law passed away in the Philippines. He celebrated my Mum's funeral.

In almost all of the weddings and funerals we sang at, he was the main celebrant. Every time he heard the song 'One Desire', he would come and see us at the end of the Mass and say to us, "I would like that song One Desire when I go home ..."

Many times he repeated this request and I would always say, "Father, you are too young to go home."

God has His ways. We did not expect Father to go in 2013. Father John was exemplary in living the Gospel of Jesus Christ. He was always loving, kind and forgiving. He always saw goodness in every situation. He was not very hard to please. He trusted our gifts and talents in the way we ministered to the Lord and His people through music. I used to be bothered by comments that our music is loud or the songs were inappropriate and if I asked his opinion he kindly said, "Tes, if some parishioners cannot appreciate your music, I encourage them to attend another Mass. All is well, don't you worry."

We witnessed how he was part of us when we had karaoke at our home. He got a score of 99, the highest score, beating Rey and my brother-in-law

Boy. He was so very pleased with his achievement. He was our karaoke king!

Father John was such a humble and a very simple man, always welcoming; a man with a very big, joyful and generous heart despite his challenges.

We felt his pain when he lost his Mum, then his Dad; then he left Narre Warren parish soon after his father's death. We know how much he suffered when he left Narre Warren Parish and the people he dearly loved and served, but as the song goes, "If I could have one desire, before my life is through, even in my darkest night my light would shine for you ..."

Father John really lived his life for our Lord Jesus. His light shone for Jesus even in the darkest and most painful times of his life. We will always remember Father John Allen who loved and served each one of us in his own unique ways for God's greater glory.

Father John, we believe you are with our Lord Jesus Christ, the One whom you have always desired to serve in your life. We love and miss you. We will miss your Sunday homilies - simple and down-to-earth but very encouraging, inspiring and spirit-filled - your presence, your smile and your stories and your precious moments with us in the family. The Narre Warren church is full of lovely memories of you. Our hearts are full of beautiful memories of you. Thank you for being part of our lives. We know you are happy where you are, singing joyful songs to the Lord with the angels and saints. And yes of course, you are His karaoke king, beating every angel and saint! Love you always.

- *Tes & Rey Halili and family.*

Much more than a priest

We are Cathy and Val, members of Our Lady Help of Christians Parish, Narre Warren, but most importantly, we are friends of John. To us he was much more than a Parish Priest. He was a good friend, who shared meals with us often, always punctuated by lively conversation.

We visit Lakes Entrance regularly and know very well the place that John called home. On his first visit to our home he was delighted to see on the wall aerial views of Lakes. Cathy had taken the photos on a joy flight over the district some years earlier. "I know where that is," he said with his big smile.

Cathy says:

One of my loveliest memories of John happened during my darkest days when I had no energy, even to get dressed. Going to Mass was, at times, just too hard, requiring more faith than I had in me. I spoke to John during Reconciliation, explaining exactly how I was feeling, stating that although "come as you are" was my anchor, I did not feel it would include me arriving at Mass in my blue nightgown, pink dressing gown and fluffy slippers. John replied that although God and he would understand, it might be shocking to the rest of the congregation. He said it in that engaging manner of his, which caused me to smile. John noticed and said, "There's a smile!"

Each time a smile occurred he remarked on it. By the time our conversation concluded I had smiled often and felt accepted, loved and knew that there would be better days eventually. And there were, and still are!

Following this conversation I had regular meeting with John in his office. He made a great cup of tea!

During the times when I found it difficult to go to Mass, it was John's homilies that somehow always seemed to manage to cover the particular worry or problem that I had at the time. It was John who suggested that I sit in the front pew so that my tears would not be noticed. I cried often but John brought me peace and gradually I have learned to live and trust once more.

My dear friend John knew me very well. There was to be a pilgrimage to the Holy Land and I wrestled with the idea of going. I asked John for his advice. His answer was gentle.

"It will entail long days, short nights with little sleep and lots of walking," he said. "Are you well enough? Think about it."

I did, and decided that it would be best to stay home where I had the comfort of friends and John.

Val says:

John helped dear friend Cath through a very dark period in her life after her marriage had broken down, guiding her through the lengthy process of annulment. Thanks to John's friendship, Cathy has slowly regained her hold on life. John also led the way to my conversion to Catholicism.

I brought Cathy into my home when she became very ill with clinical depression and severe panic attacks. I knew she could no longer live on her own if she was to survive.

I was brought up in the Anglican faith but all my life I questioned that denomination's origins. So over time, the precious earth and nature in all its forms became my 'church'.

When Cathy came to my home I drove her to Mass whenever she wanted/needed to go. At that time it seemed that her church was the only constant in her life for her.

I always remember the response from Deacon Tony Aspinall when I phoned to ask for help for Cathy. His attention was immediate. On a number of occasions I drove Cath to meet with John for some comfort and peace, which she always received.

I came to realize that Our Lady Help of Christians Parish was full of love and caring, all emanating from John.

I began attending Mass with Cath and then one day I decided to 'join up'.

I was welcomed to the faith officially in December 2005 with John officiating. It was very special and very personal as there was only me and one other taking part.

John was already close to Cathy and I knew him well at this stage and so it was easy to say, "Come and share a meal with us."

He did. And has done many times since.

I remember his first visit very well. Our dog, Molly, was little more than a puppy and she bounced all over him while he tried to defend himself against the boisterous little pooch who nicked off with his handkerchief that she pinched from his pocket! We all had a good laugh.

Cathy and I travel every year in my caravan and wherever we went John was first to receive a postcard.

We had a great time in the Clare Valley, South Australia, after John suggested we visit Sevenhills Winery. St Ignatius Merlot was on the table the next time he came for tea.

John dined with us the evening before he was to visit his doctor for his first scan. We were devastated when we discovered that he had cancer. We were so glad we could communicate with him via 'Joffa's Website'.

We continued to send him letters and cards and I put together a book of photographs I had taken of Lakes Entrance so he could have Lakes with him wherever he was.

Father Brendan brought John to our home for tea in April 2013. That was John's last visit. We will always talk about 'John's chair' in our kitchen and 'John's chair' at the table. We have been blessed by his presence in our homes and in our lives. We will always miss him. We spend quite a lot of time at Lakes every year. It was John's home and there, he is everywhere.

We have been so privileged to have known John and are grateful for this opportunity to tell some of our story with 'our John'.

He lived his faith

What did Father John contribute to our lives?

He was holy, kind, empathetic and caring.

He was a man of great passion and faith and these talents shone out of him whenever he was in the room.

He married us, baptised our babies and gave them their First Holy Communion and the Sacraments and he was instrumental in our family's faith journey.

Father John held Mum's hand in the dying hours of her life and comforted her, a lovely lady, whom I know John loved as a faithful parishioner.

Father John was a big, round bloke with white hair and a smiling face that made him charismatic.

He loved his family and was devastated by the loss of his Mum and Dad. His grief was felt by the entire congregation.

Father John was a wonderful priest and he is what Catholicism is all about. He comforted many and was loved and respected by hundreds and hundreds of people. We know he is in Heaven looking out for us all from there.

- Kathryn Lees-Doherty.

Generous and loving

We were blessed to have John as our P. P. What a beautiful man and priest! John travelled to the country for my mother's funeral Mass and also Dan's mother's Mass. Then when I was diagnosed with breast cancer in 2012, John kept in touch by phoning and leaving messages assuring me I was in his thoughts and prayers. Such a generous and loving person!

John reminded me that he had a sister called Elsie when I shared with him the news of the death of my 23-year-old niece, also named Elsie. We think of John with so much love as we grieve and remember him.

- Mary & Dan Murphy.

He made us welcome

Father John knew almost all his parishioners by name and would welcome us before Mass or sometimes afterwards. He would say, "How are you?" and usually finish with his famous phrase, "Good on you." He always had that big, big smile on his face, which made us happy, welcome and wanted.

He made us feel important as he welcomed us every Sunday, always asking after our son, Mauvin, even after he finished school and moved to the city to live. Father John's cheerfulness and humour was present in all his homilies. He always had a positive answer to every problem.

He helped us in a very special way. We came to Narre Warren from India in April 2007 and as many new migrants are, we were very depressed, homesick and had to go through many challenges. We approached Father John to seek a concession on school fees for Mauvin, who at that time was in Year XI. Father John willingly wrote a letter to the Principal of Beaconsfield Secondary College and as a result we were granted that special concession in fees. This was such a bonus to us because it made our life easier in the first two years of our new life in Australia. We cannot forget the favour he did for us and we will always remember him. We are sure he is in heaven rejoicing and praying for us.

- Lourdina & Mark Rego.

How we miss him

Father John, Father John, dear Father John
How we miss your presence here with us
You gave Him your life
You taught us how to love
Oh! How we miss you today

To Jesus you gave
All your freedom and will
You were the shepherd of us
In parishes in Sale

Now to Him you are gone
Our creator and King
Where there is no pain

With Mum and Dad who await you there
And the choirs of angels and saints
You can praise and glorify Him forevermore.

- Ashley Burrows.

Always with a smile

Father John Allen – three words to describe him: friendly, great and warm.

Father John was a wonderful priest, a great person and a thorough gentleman who always greeted you with a smile. He had a commendable memory and called everyone by first name. His Sunday homilies were always outstanding, educative and informative with a touch of humour that made it all the more appealing to celebrate the Holy Eucharist with him once a week.

We've known Father John since 2007 and the few years he was part of our lives are memories we will always reminisce about with pride and joy. We are proud that we had him in our lives and had the joy of sharing his rich wisdom.

He shared our bereavement and celebrated Mass in memory of my mum even though he was grieving for his own dad. In his simplicity he shared our bad and good times too. He gave the sacraments of First Holy Communion and Reconciliation to our daughters and of course personally blessed our home with his special prayers.

Father John is never forgotten in our household. It was an honour to have him in our lives and we will cherish the memories forever. We remember him on his birthday and he always received a birthday text from us. Ironically his name is still on my mobile list of contacts – it feels like if I delete it I will lose his blessings! I pray for his dear soul every day in my prayers for the deceased family and friends.

RIP Father John, you will never be forgotten.

- Suzan Titus.

Kind and welcoming

Edna, my 80-year-old mother-in-law, attended Mass in another parish when she had one of her legs amputated. Due to a few complications she was in a wheelchair.

I approached Father John, explaining the situation and asking about bringing her to our parish.

He said, "Bring her to Mass with you and I will personally take Communion to her in church."

We brought her and that is exactly what had happened.

Edna was so grateful that she kept coming to our church, until her passing five years ago.

You know what? He was a fantastic priest, and we do miss him.

- Keith & Hyacinth Thomasz.

Loved his footy

I felt quite close to Father John and enjoyed his football commentaries each Sunday. I knew he loved football and Essendon, of course. So much so that each year for his birthday I gave him a footy birthday card with a famous footy player on the front.

One year the card had a badge on it and you wouldn't believe it, the next day after he received the card Father John was wearing the badge on his shirt! I was so amused! I miss him dearly.

- Jenny McKillop (Meares).

A family remembers

John was one of 10 children of Jack and Therese. He was surrounded by siblings, cousins, nieces and nephews who all loved him as a person and appreciated him as a priest.

Here they reminisce on the John they fondly remember.

Ten kids, what gives?

You're one of ten?
Come again!
That's unbelievable
Inconceivable
How did your poor mother cope?
Did she tie you together with a long rope?
Theresa took it in her stride
In fact, it gave her great sense of pride
She was healthy and strong, she must have been
In her home she was undisputed queen
When she and Jack began there was only two
Ten months later out of the blue
Margaret arrived to make it three
The first branch of the family tree
Then came Elsie, number four

Hardly was she through the door
When came the twins, bonny with curls
The parents so proud of their four little girls
Then oh boy, what joy!
Blessed by God with a baby boy
It didn't stop there Maureen arrived
How on earth would they survive?
Theresa coped and besides
When God sends, God provides!
Then another lad
For his dad
The whole family thought it great
When Mary arrived, number eight
Nobody ever could possibly have foreseen
That Eileen would come upon the scene
They sat back thinking job was done
Then, by Gad, another son
I'm too old for this, Theresa lamented
Any more kids and I'll be demented
Let's stop there at half a score
Thank you God I want no more

- E. J.

The central force, shining brightly

Until very recently there were nine planets in our solar system (sorry Pluto!) all spinning around the sun's large gravitational force. When I think about my Uncle John, and his role in the Allen family's 10 siblings, I imagine him as the sun right there in the middle - calm, dependable and always able to shine sunlight onto those he came in contact with, with the other nine hurtling around him in their own orbits, somehow all interlinked and connected by this central force.

This role wasn't because he was the oldest and demanded this position but came about because of his many qualities that made him a great brother, son, uncle and priest. The ability to listen, reflect, negotiate and resolve conflict with gentle good humour. Humour that sometimes was at his own expense! But always giving his whole self to the person he was with at the time.

Being a priest also made him the central point of so many extended family celebrations. Those great life-changing events that are marked by people gathering and undertaking rituals that help celebrate the great times, such as births and marriages, and give solace in the hard times such as funerals.

When it came time for my husband Carl and I to formalise our relationship, after years of 'shacking up', it was John who officiated at our ceremony. Carl came from a family who were deeply suspicious of religion and all those who were affiliated with it. So he was intrigued to meet my uncle 'the priest'. We live in an age where there is still so much mystery, but at the same time denunciation of religion, particularly the Catholic Church. We met. Carl and he talked cricket and football and John gave him a quiet ribbing about being a Pom and a West Ham United supporter.

After John left, Carl turned to me and said, "He was just so normal!"

I don't know what he was expecting but I think that reaction in some ways summed up John's approach to life and religion. He bought normality and humour to Catholicism and any ceremony that he presided over. He made people laugh, and think, and want to come back to listen to what he had to say.

I am so pleased that we were married by John, and that we chose to have all four of our children baptised and welcomed into the family by him. Our youngest's baptism was the last time that John pulled on his robes, to welcome Jonty (Little John) into this sprawling clan of ours. Our Jonty seems to have the same big build as John and loves a ball as much as he did. I just hope that he develops some of John's humour, wisdom and charisma too.

And so it was at John's funeral that the Allen family endured that first of those life-changing events without him there to guide people through. All those planets spinning around without that presence in the middle to create order and stability. He will be dearly missed by many.

- *Tessa (Johnstone) Wilson.*

The middle child

In our birth family of 10 children, John sat exactly in the middle at Number 5. He was the linchpin that joined the younger and older groups. To the four younger siblings he was a highly esteemed and respected older brother who had chosen the priesthood and was therefore set apart to be revered and honoured. Their memories were of 'John the Priest'.

To Maureen, the next sibling in line, he was a playmate and confidante. She shared a precious brother/sister bond, a shared history.

To us four older sisters he was our little brother. We had known and cared for him since birth and understood him well. Sometimes better than he did himself!

When John started school I was 10 years old and it was my job to get him dressed and ready for the day, to hold his hand across the road and to collect him at home time. When I was teaching down the line I would collect him in my blue Corolla for a weekend at home, away from boarding college. Before he joined the seminary we enjoyed road trips together in the holidays.

So I felt privileged that he spent much of his last months in my home where I could care for him in a way our mother would have done, providing him with a safe and peaceful haven in the city where he could begin the journey to his God. It seemed right. My husband Graeme was more than happy to help him pass the long evenings by watching and discussing the late night sport on television. Trevor brought over 'Big Chair' and he felt right at home. We miss him.

- E. J.

John overboard

An enduring part of our family story is the tale of 'John Overboard' as related to me by each and every one of my older siblings, bar John - he and I both being central to the story. At the time I was about six weeks old and John two years of age and we had gone on a family picnic up the lake while Dad was doing his shrimping. He had anchored the 'Erin' with Mum and all the kids on board (Margaret, Elsie, Kathleen, Joan, John and me, baby Maureen) to wait for him as he set off in the dinghy to lift the shrimp nets. Dad was well out of reach when calamity struck! Mum was nursing me when, with a quick head count, the alarm bells sounded – one child short!

"Where is John???"

Well, without a thought for my delicate age and constitution, Mum "dropped me on my head" and dived overboard to collect little John from where he was lying on the bottom of the lake. She was not a swimmer by any stretch of the imagination, however, her courage prevailed and she emerged from the deep, clear water triumphant with the little fellow in hand. For Mum, this miracle was a sure sign that God had big plans for her precious little boy! It also set in concrete her intense dislike for any activities related to the water. In my conscious memory, her anxieties prevented her from any further participation in aquatic adventures. As for me, to this day we will probably never know for sure just how much lasting damage I suffered when Mum "dropped me on my head"!

John didn't seem to be very much affected by this experience in the long term because he loved the beach, loved to go body surfing, enjoyed boating and many of his holiday destinations were by the water. He loved Lakes Entrance and the call of the water was always strong in his heart, though he learned to treat it with the respect that is its due.

- *Maureen (Allen) Santamaria.*

My cultural education

Being hemmed in by two brothers in the middle of our family wasn't necessarily the way a little girl would have planned it – but as fate would have it, that is what I was gifted with. Now, boys are not very useful for playing 'dress-ups' as princesses nor are they very forthcoming in playing 'mothers and fathers' and taking orders from their sister. And so it was that for me to have anyone to play with I had to at least try to join in their games. These ranged from 'cowboys and indians', where we would set up a tent in the backyard and camp out in it until we were so scared of the dark we'd come into our own beds - usually about 10 pm when the treats had all been eaten! - to 'cops and robbers' with a variety of arsenals including popguns, potato guns and cap guns. Then there were the inevitable football and cricket matches, which filled many hours over the school holidays. Football was not such a problem because John was able to play single-handed – he'd do the umpire's job bouncing the footy on the concrete, go up in the ruck, grab it and bounce his way up the imaginary field before finally delivering a beautiful drop punt through the goal posts! This was all commentated by himself, and the 'hero' was of course an Essendon player of the day - Alan Noonan or Ken Fletcher or someone of that calibre, he knew them all. It did provide some entertainment for the casual listener.

Cricket, however, was not so easy! For starters I simply didn't understand the finer aspects of the game.

The television and the radio both got a good workout when the Test matches were on and John would disappear into the lounge room where there were long periods of quiet interspersed with an occasional roar of "He's out!", the house rocking on its foundations as he leapt into life.

It seemed to me that in order to play the game you needed to have at a minimum, a batsman and a bowler, and some lackey who would chase the ball and return it to the bowler. That was where I came in! John and Arthur had it all sewn up – they would let me play with them and of course I was the fieldsman. After what seemed to me an eternity one of them would get 'out' and the other would then be 'in' for another eternity. I asserted my right to a bat and would generally be clean bowled on the first ball, which would have measured about 100 kmh at least. Or so it seemed to an eight year old. Anyway, it really didn't seem much fun at all!

At many of our family gatherings the old cricket match was centrepiece of the day and some fond memories remain. One in particular was a family picnic at Eureka in Ballarat, a beautiful treed area where we set up in the shade and enjoyed a lovely time talking, eating, drinking and playing together. When it came time for the match it became obvious that there were certain adjustments to the regulations that had to be made in the interests of fair play and spectator interest. One problem in particular was the trees - beautiful for their generous proportions and lush shade, but unfortunately making it too easy for a player to be caught out as the ball tangled with the branches. So the rules evolved to rectify this anomaly – first you had to catch the ball with one hand. This really did not make too much difference with the amazing talent on show and so a second complicating requirement was inserted; the fieldsman catching the ball in one hand also had to be hopping. Well, you know we had some very fine, seasoned cricketers on the field that day and a few catches were taken before it was decided that the rules needed to be revised to truly address the bias against the batsmen. And so, the final extra degree of difficulty for a valid catch was that the fieldsman had not only to catch the ball with one hand whilst hopping on one leg, but he had to be reciting the 'Hail Mary' at the same time! And who was the man of the match? The cheers and adulation flowed as John, demonstrating his skill, dexterity and sporting prowess, took a regulation catch. There may have been some divine intervention, but it was definitely spectacular and went down in family folklore as the catch of the century!

- Maureen (Allen) Santamaria.

Santa Claus is coming tonight

Christmas is such an exciting time for little children with so many wonderful thoughts filling their heads. Our four children always fondly remember Christmas Eve as the highlight of their lives.

The day was usually warm and the buzz was almost at a fever pitch with the Christmas tree decorated with pretty lights and tinsel and mysterious gifts wrapped and placed temptingly under the tree. The last postal delivery arrived with eager children running in with the mail to open up the beautiful Christmas cards, and it was well nigh impossible to coax them into having an afternoon sleep so that they could enjoy the open air Mass at St James Primary School.

At 7 pm the young shepherds, wise men, Mary and Joseph and a choir of angels all gathered on the oval, as the Mass Centre was not large enough to cater for the numbers. Mass felt so different out in the open and as singing filled the evening air, neighbours from all around came to join in our lovely celebration. The little children sang 'Away In A Manger' with their beautiful eyes so full of wonder and anticipation. As we moved to go home to settle down for the night, we heard the bellbirds in the distance, a sure reminder that Santa's sleigh was on its way!

Meanwhile back at Morwell, John would be preparing for his Christmas Eve Mass. It was the most special night for him too, and he delighted in the number of people who filled the church and the little children who were all starry eyed with the wonder of it all. As soon as he returned home between Masses, he'd be on the phone to wish us all a Happy Christmas. It was common knowledge that John had some special connection, not only with God but with all things invisible, and this included Santa Claus and so he would speak with each child and let them know just how close Santa was getting. There would be a series of two or three updates on his progress.

"He's just left Morwell and is on his way to Moe so you'd better get into bed now," he would start with.

The next one would be a little more urgent.

"What aren't you in bed yet? He's getting closer, Dominic, so he won't come if you're not in bed. Quick, get into bed!"

The final call would come with the current location of the sleigh being Mitcham – far too close for comfort and definitely not worth pushing your luck! So off to bed they would run again, and this time they'd stay there.

Sure enough, in what seemed to us parents like just a couple of minutes the children would wake up, the sun creeping over the horizon, and Santa had already been and gone, off to deliver his gifts to all the other children in the world.

My children always knew that John had a direct line to Santa Claus, no question about that. We felt so very special that we were the only people we knew who had access to this privileged information, ensuring that all were tucked up in bed and didn't miss out on Santa Claus coming.

I'm certain he absolutely delighted in this annual ritual, joining in the excitement of the kids and reliving his own childhood Christmas dreams. This was one of the really lovable traits John had – he was always in touch with his inner child and this enabled him to relate to little people in a playful yet sincere way. All the kids really loved him and have such happy memories to cherish.

- Maureen (Allen) Santamaria.

More than a brother

John was a special brother to me, always there to support, love and encourage me.

I have so many special memories. The nail-care kit he gave me for my 13th birthday, visiting him at the seminary, R. E. camps, celebrating my

Graduation Mass at St V's, meals with him in Melbourne, staying with him, those great double roasts we would have when he came home, nights at home in front of the fire watching TV with Mum and Dad, driving to Bruthen at night to pick him up from his Christmas job, the drone of the cricket commentary in summer, him teaching me it wasn't appropriate to knit throughout the Essendon football at Windy Hill, waiting for him to arrive home for Christmas lunch, looking forward to his annual visit to Perth, easing my burden of being away from Mum and Dad because he was always there looking out for them, caring for them and filling their lives with love and joy. I appreciate that so much.

I thank him for marrying us and for making it such a special day, for welcoming my husband to the family and for being such a special uncle to my children. He was very special to them.

I thank him for all he did to nurture their path. I thank him for tempering my sometimes emotional responses and for all the special and treasured gifts he gave me over the years.

John was more than a brother to me. Whenever I think of Mum and Dad, it always goes, "Mum, Dad and John."

My heart is heavy but full of love. I know that God has His protective arms around John and has him in His care.

- Eileen (Allen) Paparo.

Important to our lives

John was a special brother for my wife and a really important part of our children's lives. They have always loved John's presence, his great sense of humour and his great commitment to our faith and to the Bombers! He was a really important part of my life also.

- Jim Paparo.

The rock

John was a treasured member of our family, the centre, the rock. He was loving and generous in spirit, dependable, uncomplicated, loyal and dutiful. He told me before he died that every day of his life for as long as he could remember, he tried to be the very best man he could be. He died without an enemy. There were one or two people he had disagreements with but he had made his peace, forgiven and was on good terms with them when he passed to his eternal reward. We will miss him always.

- Mary (Allen) Keeley.

A living memory

Dear John, I find myself thinking about you during the quiet times in my day. My mind mulls over the place you occupy in my life. You are my uncle, the man who baptised and welcomed me into our family's faith, the man who married me to the most wonderful man, my mother's precious brother and my daughters' great uncle. I remember with warmth a particular Christmas when we lived in Melbourne. It was sunset and we were all outside in the front yard saying goodbye to some friends that had come for supper after Mass. There was a big streak across the sky and Mum told us that it was the tracks of Santa's sleigh. With that she took us inside and called you on the phone to check how far away Santa was. It seemed common knowledge at home, that because you were a priest, you had a direct line to Santa and was privy to his movements and knew his estimated time of arrival at our place. So, after learning that he was not far away and that he wouldn't come unless we were asleep, we quickly got into our pyjamas and got into bed. I never questioned that you knew Santa personally.

I remember clearly a visit from you when we had just moved to Ballarat. We lived beside the school and you were on a recruitment mission. You offered me my own footy jumper and scarf on condition that I converted my allegiance to the Bombers. I was seriously considering the position and thinking that I probably looked better in red than in navy blue when Dad got word of what was happening and put the hard word on me. He told me that if I lived under his roof I had to be a Blues girl. You nearly had me!

In the lead up to my marriage you were a source of gentle and wise guidance. It was most important to me that you be the celebrant of my marriage and it was not easy to convince my partner that we be married in a church. With your gentle and understanding approach you were able to alleviate his concerns and make our marriage most meaningful. It was wonderful to have a man who had known me since I was born to officiate the joining of my life to my chosen partner. A privilege that most people do not get to experience! Thank you.

You will be a living memory in my home, talked about and remembered. Whenever we watch the footy, reminisce on Christmas Eve, talk about our wedding day and get together with extended relatives, you will be with us.

As I hold my baby in my arms and look down at her sleeping face I think about how Nanna would have held you and looked at you in just the same way. With the same intensity of love and wonder! The wonder of life and beyond. I know that Nanna will be waiting for you, to be all that you need her to be. Thank you for being in my life. I love you.

- *Erin (Santamaria) Dawson.*

That Bomber's dressing gown!

I miss my dear uncle so much. Losing him made me realise what a special role he played in my life, and the lives of all my cousins too. John was the uncle who attended every event and took an interest in everything you were doing. I have special memories of driving down to Lakes with John and listening to his amazing CD collection. Taking

John out to the opera and hearing his snores in perfect harmony with the orchestra! Just the fact that when down in Lakes, Uncle John would always be there on a Monday morning in his Bombers dressing gown drinking a cuppa and reading the paper. I miss him so much. He was such a blessing.

- Elise Keeley.

My godfather

John, what a journey you have been on! Your dedication to our family and the communities that you have served will never be forgotten. You have touched many people's lives in such a positive way. I will always treasure you as my uncle, my Godfather and the most loyal Bombers supporter. I remember the time that you were literally frothing at the mouth over them losing. Know that my thoughts and love are with you always.

- Brendan Allen.

The things we did for John!

There I was, sitting in the back of the car, an impressionable eight-year-old with a Discman and a Tina Arena CD ready to go on a summer holiday. Packed, excited, all set for the beach.

Then something got in the back seat with me that ruined my entire journey. It repulsed me. It went against everything I believed in Even the dulcet tones of Ms Arena couldn't take my mind off what was next to me.

A life-sized cut-out of James Hird!

It was a birthday present for my uncle, Father John Allen, and I had the 'pleasure' of sitting next to it all the way to his house in Narre Warren.

John was very thankful for the gift when we arrived and managed to extract Jimmy from the back seat.

Sitting next to that floppy haircut and smug smile for an hour was, I suppose, a small thing I could do for John, who did so much for the Allen family. After Nanna and Gugga died, Uncle John was the heart of the Allen family. He was a crucial link between all generations.

As he didn't have any children of his own, all his nieces and nephews felt like they were his children. John always made the effort to come to special occasions - most of the time he presided over them. Births, marriages and deaths! John added his own special presence to all ceremonies. He was a man of humour, humanity and honour.

Growing up you think it's normal to have a priest in the family. It was only as I grew older that I realised how special, and unusual, it was.

I hope Uncle John is resting well up their behind those pearly white gates. I can just imagine him now having a cup of tea with Nanna and Gugga.

He'd be sitting in a big, comfy recliner with a hearty meal, and be, of course, surrounded by cut-outs of Essendon legends.

- Eloise Johnstone.

Holidays with John

Some of my great memories with John involve drives from Melbourne to Lakes listening to the best music! And he knew all the best places to stop along the way, and knew most of the people at the cafes too. I'm pretty sure that the first time I ever tried a Magnum ice-cream was in Broome with John. He knew how to make holidays fun! And he was the one that introduced us to 'Grease, the Musical'! We watched that VCR to death and I think of him whenever I sing any of the 'Grease' songs.

- Therese (Keeley) Brookes.

Personal touch

John, you have given so much to so many over such a long period of time. As a family we have been truly blessed by having a personal touch at so many of the important milestones in our lives. It is time now for you to fall back into the abundant love and goodwill that surrounds you. We stand ready to do anything that we can do to help at this time; nothing is too big or small, if there is anything we can help with please just let us know.

- Bryan & Trudi Ross.

John's visits

I remember when I was in Year 1 and Uncle Johnny came to visit us in Perth. He asked me about what I like at our school canteen; I said choc-milks. Each day he was there he gave me money for a choc-milk. I always remember how generous and kind-hearted Uncle Johnny was. I also loved how passionate Johnny was about his football; it's probably the main reason I love football so much now! Uncle John had always wanted to make sure that I was going for Essendon. He even gave me an Essendon scarf and beanie one birthday, AND a signed Matthew Lloyd poster. Although my loyalties lie with the Dockers, I'll always have a soft spot for the Bombers.

- Laura Keeley.

John was fabulous

When I think about my Uncle John it is both with a heavy heart and a smile on my face. He was such a lovely man, one that I am privileged to have known and loved.

I remember times at my grandparent's house when John, Eileen and Robert all still lived there. They loved razzing each other up like all brothers and sisters do, which made for some hilarious Sunday morning teas after Sunday Mass.

I went to St Brendan's Primary School and when our parish priest Father Shanley was away, John would often replace him. This was always great because we got to see him every day and because we could boast to all the other kids that he was our uncle.

On the other hand it was a little awkward because it meant we had to go and say our weekly confession to him! I dreaded weekly confession as it was, just repeating the same 'sins', such as not making my bed or fighting with my sisters, but John was fabulous. He never got me to confess my sins but I just sat beside him and had a little chat about Mum and Dad, my sisters Trudi and Michelle, and of course football!

I remember his love and devotion to Essendon. He was so passionate when it came to them and would never have a bad word said about them without a witty comeback.

My dad Laurie is an equally passionate Carlton supporter and they always had a dig at each other. Dad is certainly not a prayerful man but I think even he resorted to praying when Carlton played Essendon. Of course, a phone call from John always followed when the Bombers beat the Blues but it was ominously quiet if the Bombers were toppled, much to Dad's delight!

My mum Joan recalls John crying at a very young age when the Bombers lost, so it was certainly a long-standing love he had for them.

Apparently John didn't always have a calm and reverent manner about him and if things didn't go his way as a child, he would drop down to the floor, totally lose the plot and spin around on his back! Mum remembers the family calling that "the flat spin."

John was involved in every birth, death and marriage in our family. Not many people have the privilege of a priest in the family and it gave all of our christenings, weddings and funerals a really personal touch

On my own wedding day I remember how special it was to have John marry us. It was a special moment walking down the aisle and seeing the pride and joy on John's face and how proud he was to be an integral part of our special day. He put his own spin on it as only John could, giving us a few giggles and if I remember correctly, he even had a dig at Marty for barracking for the Blues! And once the formalities were over he partied it up with the rest of us enjoying a wine and a dance.

John also christened our two boys, Jack and Archie. We were living in Sunbury at the time and weren't regular churchgoers. John knew this but was never judgmental. He was just rapt to be able to christen his grand nephews. We had chosen my uncles Robert and Roger to be the boys' godparents and I asked John if it was okay to have two male godparents.

"Of course it is Nicole," John said. "I couldn't think of two better people."

This just shows how accepting and loving John was of everyone. But a few days before the ceremony, we received a call from the Sunbury Parish Priest letting us know that this was not allowed. I was devastated and explained that these were our two people of choice and that my uncle, Father John Allen, was conducting the service and he had assured me it was okay. Once I mentioned John's name, the priest did a complete '180' and said, "Well, if John says it's okay, then it's okay!"

I think this shows the esteem in which his peers held him. We went on to have a great service and a beautiful gathering afterwards, all thanks to John. That day, he gave Marty and me a beautiful nativity scene that will forever take pride of place amongst all of our Christmas decorations.

When John was diagnosed with pancreatic cancer, we were all shocked and devastated. The prognosis was never going to be good. It still astounds me to this day how gracefully John handled his diagnosis. I often had conversations with my husband Marty about how wrong I thought it was that he had devoted his life so wholeheartedly to his faith and this was the outcome.

Clearly John was a lot more philosophical than me and seemed to accept the inevitable. Whenever I asked how he was going he would say, "I'm going fine, Nicole, certainly better than yesterday."

I don't think he ever burdened anyone with the pain he clearly must have been suffering.

But that was John to a tee. He was always the sort of a man that I hope my two boys will turn out to be.

He put his all into his time on this earth, mainly for the greater good of others. He was always a selfless, endearing, hard-working man who would never fail to keep up to date with all the goings-on of his much loved brothers, sisters, in-laws, nieces and nephews. I think of him and miss him daily and I just hope his beloved Bombers can get up this year and we hear him cheering from the heavens. Just don't tell my Dad!

- Nicole (Appleby) Donovan.

Always had time for family

Father John Allen was known to me as my cousin John. He was a wonderful cousin, always at the end of the phone ready to make time, pleased to see me when I dropped in on my way back to Sale. I was often knocking on his door to say "Hi", as my first year away from home was difficult and he knew how homesick I was. I received my first bouquet of flowers from John on my 21st birthday. Wow, was I thrilled!

John was my Lakes Entrance cousin. Lakes was a long way from Melbourne, but when John came to Melbourne to live with Aunty Eily in Albert Park, when I was a young child, the relationship really began. I got to know John as there was always a Canning sleeping over at Eily's house. John must have stayed with her a lot as he had a room assigned especially to him that was known as 'John's room'.

John was loved by our family and was a significant part in our lives. My mum Agnes and her sister Eily thought he was wonderful and therefore we did also. John really was wonderful! He was a very warm person and must have been very skilled at developing strong bonds, as I always felt connected to him.

As a child we would visit him at Werribee Mansion. I thought we went lots but I think now John was only there for twelve months as the seminary was later moved to Clayton. However, I remember those visits vividly - John would be wearing his long robe looking so regal and important. He was always so pleased to see us and ever so grateful for the visit.

I remember clearly John being ordained a priest. We made the long journey from Melbourne to Sale, mum having packed nine individual chicken and salad dinners in margarine containers to eat on the way. It was a wonderful celebration and the party afterwards was a feast.

John was always there for us. He married all of my brothers and sisters, and baptised some of our children. As his own immediate family was extending and many of his nieces and nephews were having children, I didn't like to pull on John's time, as he was the parish priest of one of the largest parishes in Australia. When I was preparing for the baptism of my third child, I didn't ask John to baptise her and I remember him clearly saying to me that he always had time for family! Family was important to him. That was the sort of man he was. He made time for everyone and made us feel important.

My own wedding day was a perfect example of this. The photographer wanted the wedding at 2 pm so that we would have good light. I rang John and asked him whether that would be all right. Without hesitation he said 'yes'. It wasn't until years later that I realised how much pressure that actually put John under. Being a Sunday, he probably said the 11 am Mass and most likely didn't get out of the church until 12.30 pm. It would have been a huge rush for him to eat lunch and travel to Middle Park. Not once was that reflected back to me. That was the sort of person John was. My wedding was beautiful! John was wonderful and what a special memory that is for me to have of him.

My mum got very sick and was admitted to hospital for major surgery. As soon as John heard, he was there. He gave her the sacrament for Anointing of the Sick. I found it very emotional. Mum knew how sick she was but it soothed her and gave her the extra courage to fight on. Once again John was there.

When Mum finally did pass away of course John was there to support us all. Her farewell was such a beautiful celebration of her life and John was the one who made it come alive by holding the whole thing together.

With Mum gone, the family link with her side of the family could have changed, but John made sure that it didn't happen. He always dropped in on Dad to have a cuppa when he was in Melbourne.

John came especially to tell Dad about his own sickness. He was strong and family-minded to the end. A couple of days before he died, he asked to see my father again as he wanted to say his last farewell to us as a family. It was so special for us all. It was so significant and wonderful for us to all know that John felt we were important. It was a mutual love; he was family.

Our memories are vivid and warm. He was taken from us when he had so much more to give but he used his time wisely on this earth, making people the focus. I am so grateful that I shared a part of it.

- Therese (Canning) John.

When Uncle John plucked one from heaven

Time - My childhood.

Place - A wide open parkland.

Event - An Allen family get together (always a big affair).

I can still smell the mixture of insect repellent, sunscreen and lush grass. The whole clan had been playing cricket for quite some time, with countless aunties, cousins and uncles standing and chattering in the field.

One of my more competitive relatives had smacked the tennis ball into the trees a couple of times in succession, which prompted an emergency on-field discussion about the rules. The consensus: If the ball hits a tree, the fielder must catch the ball in one hand, whilst hopping on one foot, reciting the Hail Mary.

The very next delivery, the batsman (it was either one of my older male cousins, or an uncle) whacked the ball with some serious venom towards a pine tree. In an instant, the ball pinged at an impossible angle off the tree and straight into the outstretched left hand of Uncle John! Before we could even appreciate this amazing feat of reflex and coordination, John was already reciting his prayers whilst hopping on one foot, leaving the whole gathering in fits of laughter.

It was the best catch I have ever seen in cricket, and one of my favourite memories.

- Chris Johnstone.

Glory and anxiety on and off the footy field

Football played a huge part in John's life. No only did he love the Bombers he devoured every word on the back pages of the papers and absorbed every TV sports show. Winning the flag was everything and he tasted premiership success himself. But if you failed to measure up to John's stringent standards - even wearing the red and black - then God have mercy on you.

Joffa and the boys win the big one!

While John loved footy with a passion, even he acknowledged that he was not the most skilful exponent of the game. Perhaps a little slow off the mark and lacking just a bit of depth with his hallmark wonky left-foot kicks, he made up for it with a very solid presence, a fierce determination bordering on frothing anger, and a well-rehearsed crash tackle. But the thing was, he achieved something that the rest of us mug footballers in those days would have died for – a premiership.

John played on the wing for the Corpus Christi seminary side at Clayton in the mid-70s. A somewhat original collection of eclectic misfits, they probably would not have worried the better sides in their suburban league if not for their sheer enthusiasm, dogged persistence and two secret weapons. One was a young Vietnamese seminarian named Bart who, brand new to the Australian game, consistently confounded the opposition with his crazy-horse style. Totally unpredictable, Bart would pirouette out of packs, leaving everyone – including himself – confused as to how he managed to snare the ball in the first place and what he was going to do with it next. Luckily he had mastered the perfect technique. The long-bomb down to the team's other secret weapon – Fitzy the Skipper.

Fitzy was a sublimely talented footballer who had shown great personal selflessness in subsuming his obvious League potential in order to serve the Lord. He had beautiful foot and hand skills, could mark anything that came his way and, like a true champion, always had all the time in the world.

Under the direction of an astute coach, the boys worked their way into the 1977 Grand Final. In a tense and exciting battle on an oval in the shadows of what was then Caulfield Institute of Technology, the young underdog seminarians clung to their older, tougher opponents throughout the day but could not quite match it with them. Then John pulled down a mark, Bart took the handball and banged it forward and Fitzy did the rest. This sparked a clutch of goals and suddenly, the boys in navy blue with the big white 'C' on their chest had hit the lead and were not going to relinquish it.

John had had an intriguing battle on the wing all day, shading his taller, skinnier opponent sporting rock-band roadie hair and just one tooth in his otherwise gummy mouth. Finally, this bloke reckoned he had figured what would put John off his game.

Pointing to the white single-letter monogram he snarled, "What does the 'C' stand for, mate? Goose ..?" Years later, we were all still trying to work that one out.

When Fitzy kicked the sealer, the tiny crowd of family and friends on the boundary went crazy, manfully doing our best to shout convincingly, "Come on Corpus!" It was generally agreed that none of us had ever barracked so enthusiastically for a dead body before in our lives ...

But, boy was it worth it. The game had been a thriller, the boys had overcome the greatest of odds, and Joffa had joined the premiership hall of fame.

Oh, he could be a harsh critic

We all know that John loved Essendon. But that did not necessarily mean he loved every Essendon player.

Certainly not Tayte Pears. The young defender might have gained an AFL Rising Star nomination, he might have held his own against forwards of the star quality of Jarryd Roughead and Brendan Fevola, and he might be considered by the Bombers as a "huge part of Essendon's future." But John only ever had one word for him. "Useless!"

The poor boy only had to go near the ball and John was out of the chair and on his feet, cheeks turning to his customary shade of vermilion as he gave number 16 a fearful serve. "Useless, Pears!" he would exclaim. "I dunno how he gets a game!"

Even of the poor kid got the ball, evaded three players, took two bounces and fired a lace-out pass down the throat of Jobe Watson, John would grumble, "Lucky, Pears, lucky ..."

No one is quite sure what minor error poor old Tayte made in his first couple of games that John obviously spotted and then made him a marked man, but he was not alone. Over the years there were a handful of targets who wore the red and black but who John found wanting. David Calthorpe got a regular spray, as did Dean Solomon, Adam McPhee, John Barnes and Ricky Olarenshaw.

John never felt more justified in his criticism than when they all got packed off to other clubs.

Just warning you, Tayte. If you end up in the back blocks of outer western Sydney, you will know why.

- Graeme Johnstone.

Obituary, 'The Age'

August 30, 2013

Much-loved priest who had a gift for bringing people together

Father John Allen - Parish Priest
08/11/1952 - 12/07/2013

Father John Allen was buried in the vestments of his priestly ministry that had been lovingly stitched for him by his mother and his sister-in-law on the occasion of his ordination in Sale in 1978.

In these days when the clergy in general and Catholic priests in particular receive regular negative publicity we tend to overlook the many good men who continue to dedicate their lives to preaching the gospel and ministering dutifully to their congregations. Father John Allen was one such man. A man who was loved and respected by the people whose lives he touched in many ways in times of stress and of joy.

The 1500 people who attended his Vigil Mass in Narre Warren and the 1000 that paid their respects at his funeral in his boyhood town of Lakes Entrance the following day attest to the high esteem in which he was held.

John Damien Allen was born in Bairnsdale on November 8, 1952, fifth child and eldest son of Jack and Theresa Allen of Lakes Entrance. He had nine siblings. He began primary school in Lakes Entrance on the day St Brendan's opened its doors and then went on to be educated at St Patrick's College Sale, Corpus Christi College at Werribee and Clayton, and Melbourne University.

Father John served in varying roles at Lakes Entrance, Traralgon, Sale, Yarram, Morwell, Narre Warren and Iona/Maryknoll/Koo Wee Rup. But it was at Narre Warren, where he worked for 16 years as parish priest, that he became a part of everybody's family. He made Sunday Mass a welcoming place where the multi-cultural congregation in this thriving growth corridor of Melbourne developed as one community and felt so much at home.

During his time he oversaw the establishment of primary and secondary schools and an extension of the church to accommodate the rapidly growing, diverse population. He nurtured a meeting place where the Eucharist was celebrated; new babies welcomed, young couples married and the dead buried. Our Lady Help of Christians Narre Warren is a vibrant community, a place where people from all nations meet to worship and learn what it is to be Australian. Father John had a gift with people and his personality permeated the whole parish. It is a happy place.

John's other passion was sport and he used it effectively to connect people, introducing newly arrived migrants to the wonders of Australian Rules football. He had followed Essendon since a boy and so endeavoured to recruit as many supporters as possible, engaging in good-natured banter that everyone enjoyed. In 1999 when the Blues unexpectedly beat the Bombers in the preliminary final by one point, he walked on to the altar next morning and looked up to see that the congregation had dressed in Carlton colours just to tease him! He took it well.

Many people wore red and black to his funeral and the Essendon theme song was sung as red and black balloons were released to fly off over Bass Strait. Perhaps the same way as their premiership hopes are going for 2013!

Because many of his parishioners were Indian or Sri Lankan there was also lively debate in the cricket season. As well, John was well informed on current world and local affairs and travelled extensively during his sabbaticals. He visited many places from whence his parishioners hailed as he believed that this helped him to further understand and connect. He loved to read histories and biographies, kept abreast with the latest films and was a dedicated gardener. Folklore has it that at parish functions he was also the king of karaoke.

Not many men have seven sisters, John always jokingly saying that that was one reason he became a priest. So that he could get a word in when he preached on a Sunday! He also had two brothers.

"I pray each day for the grace to strive to be the best man I possibly can," John told his sister Mary when she asked him what he prayed about.

John's loyal family sustained and supported him through his illness after he was diagnosed with pancreatic cancer in November 2012. He asked so little and gave so much to everybody who crossed his path.

The life of a priest is a solitary one where the very nature of the work both connects and separates. Father John Allen was amazingly connected and loved. "I was happy to be a priest; it is a most happy and fulfilling life," he wrote in a message penned when he knew his time had come. "To my family, friends and parishioners, who have prayed for me over all these years, you will not be forgotten in my heavenly home."

John lived a public life but in the end, he was a brother, uncle, friend and colleague, just John. He died on 12th July 2013, aged 60.

He will be greatly missed.

- Elsie Johnstone, one of John's seven sisters.

Now that he's gone

What has happened to Father John?
His body is dead, his soul has gone,
Does he live on and on and on?
Did a band of celestial creatures
Whose job it is to welcome preachers
Herald John and grant his reward
For all the sacrifices he'd endured?
Was he met at heaven's door
By all his folk who'd gone before?
Did his spirit soar and soar?
And did he at last enjoy
What he'd been promised as a boy?
And had lived his life accordingly
So that the Almighty face he'd see
In that microsecond 'tween life and death
As John breathed his final breath
It became apparent
Transparent

The ultimate truth did unfold
Alas it cannot be told
Until that inevitable day
When we come to pass away
We will confront the mystery
Of our ultimate history
Oh, how we prayed to keep him here
But God ignored our faithful prayer
Because He had another plan
Beyond what mortals understand
He headhunted John for his very own team
To welcome souls to their heavenly dream
So that we pilgrims are not alone
When we make our final trip home
You see, John's earthly skills are transferable
Both clerical and spiritual
Father John has gone before
To be there at Heaven's door
To smile and meet us
Welcome and greet us

- E. J.

www.ingramcontent.com/pod-product-compliance
Lightning Source LLC
Chambersburg PA
CBHW051045160426
43193CB00010B/1074